You Make Me Feel
Like an Unnatural Woman

DIARY OF AN NEW [OLDER] MOTHER

Judith Newman

MIRAMAX BOOKS

For information address:

Hyperion

77 West 66th Street

New York, New York 10023-6298

FIRST EDITION

10 9 8 7 6 5 4 3 2 1

The joys of parents are secret; and so are their griefs and fears. They cannot utter the one; nor they will not utter the other. Children sweeten labors; but they make misfortunes more bitter. They increase the cares of life; but they mitigate the remembrance of death.

—Francis Bacon

Carrie, to Charlotte: You have plenty of time to have children.
Charlotte: No, I don't! I don't want to be one of those forty-year-old moms!

—*Sex and the City,*
in the episode "The Baby Shower"

ACKNOWLEDGMENTS

YOU KNOW THE GUY WHO WINS AN OSCAR for, say, sound editing, who thanks so many people the award organizers need a hook to get him off the stage? I'm that guy.

To Susan Reed, the first person to think this book wasn't a stupid idea, and to Mark Reiter, my agent, who could have written it better than I have. To Jonathan Burnham at Miramax, not only for buying this book but for being too English and polite to mention over dinner how late it was.

To my Miramax editor, JillEllyn Riley. Other editors at publishing houses could learn lessons in diplomacy from JillEllyn. Before handing me her revisions on this manuscript, she said, "Judith, we're so happy. You've written something so much more ambitious than just a humor book, which of course is why we think you could make a few minor changes." This was the only thing she could have said to keep me from gouging out my eyes when I saw the actual revision notes, which consisted of Post-its on every single page in handwriting normally reserved for people who etch names on grains of rice.

Acknowledgments

To the heads of the admissions offices of Collegiate, Grace Church, St. Bernard's, Buckley, Friends, and the UN School—because it's never too early to suck up.

To Jamie Grifo, for bringing me Henry and Augustus with his science, and Machelle Seibel, for bringing me them with his prayers.

As a photographer whose specialty is fuzzy overlit close-ups of the subject's right nostril, I am particularly grateful to Diane Salvatore of *Ladies' Home Journal.* She hired me to write a monthly column about Henry and Gus—a column which required pictures. This means I have photographs of my children where they are recognizably human and don't look like they were shot by the same people who track UFOs and the Loch Ness monster.

To Steven Weinreb, whom I love, and because if I didn't thank him here I suspect I'd never hear the end of it.

To Jerrard and Sandra Siegal, the surrogate grandparents.

To Jacyln Lee: Henry and Gus think it's all been a big mistake; they know who should have been their mother. And to boy wonder/future babysitter Jack Asimov—the kind of guy I hope Henry and Gus will become.

To Lige Burroughs Rushing IV, for lessons learned.

My friends have shown me kindness beyond anything I could ever imagine. To Elizabeth Crow, who can turn the unspeakable into the unspeakably funny and who I want to grow up to be someday. To Maria Wilhelm and Nancy Kalish, who would be my sisters if I were able to choose these things. To Nigella Lawson, whose funny darkness has always been light to me. To Lisa Mienville, who shipped me her leftover fertility drugs—the ones that eventually resulted in my becoming pregnant. To Gay Daly, who convinced me that maybe I wouldn't kill my children with my incompetence before their first birthday. To Susan Wawrose, for knowing I was too cheap to buy my own maternity clothes. To Val Frankel, for making me an offer in my darkest hour that I'll never forget. To Susan McCarthy, the writer I wish I could be and the loveliest virtual friend a girl could have. To Casey Ellis, for keeping me laughing and for keeping Henry and Gus well dressed. To Amanda Lovell, Mary Lou Dinardo, Amy Scott, Laurie Lewis, Elissa Hason, Martha Barretre, Kim Johnson Gross, Jane Greer, Maria Rodriguez, Lise Olsen, and Marjorie Ingall, for listening to me complain past the point where normal people would have told me to shut up.

This is the part where you're supposed to thank your husband for all his support. Ha. Hahahahahahaha! Sometimes I crack myself up!

To my aunt, Alberta Lewis, the person who screamed at me five hundred times, *"Don't you dare mention me in your book!":* the woman with a thousand opinions and even more kindnesses. Few women are blessed with a second mother, as I've been.

These days I understand, in a way I never could, why my own mother sulked when I wouldn't celebrate my birthday with her. It was her birthday too. In a very real sense, the day we have our children is the day we are reborn.

Shortly before I turned in this manuscript my father said to me, "When you were a baby . . . that was the happiest time of my life." Now, having had babies myself, I finally know him for who he is: a crazy, crazy old man.

So this book is dedicated to my parents, Frances and Edmund. If I can be half as good a parent to Henry and Augustus as you've been to me, my sons have nothing to fear in this world.

PROLOGUE

I DON'T LIKE CHILDREN VERY MUCH. Which is how I became the mother of twins.

My sentiments are common, if unspoken. You don't become a first-time mother at forty if your attitude toward kids has always been, "Hey! Bring 'em on!" True, there are women who find they can't conceive at twenty-five who spend the next decade doing everything in their power to start a family. But these are the exceptions. The rule is a whole generation of women like me who were told we could (and should) have it all, then woke up one day in our late thirties or early forties, slapped ourselves upside the head, and said (like that famous T-shirt), *"Damn. I forgot to have a baby."* It's funny how the denial of a thing leads to desperate measures to obtain it. If diamonds were scattered on the streets, would anyone bother to pick them up?

And so the quest for the Holy Infant begins: the tests, the doctors, the sex with all the spontaneity of a military drill. The anxiety. The disappointments. And sometimes, the baby.

Or babies, plural. In 2001, the last time these statistics were gathered, 1.7 bazillion women in the United States gave birth to twins or higher-order multiples. OK, not really. The real number is more like 121,246. It only *seems* like 1.7 bazillion because they all live on my block. At any rate, the rest of this paragraph is true: Twins used to occur in one out of ninety live births. Now, thanks to fertility drugs and women's starting their families later (older mothers have a greater chance of having twins even without the drugs), the incidence is about one in thirty-four. If I spot a woman in her thirties or forties with twins, we have a shorthand conversation that goes something like, "Grifo, NYU?"

"No, Sauer, Columbia Presbyterian."

"How many cycles?"

"Third one—got lucky."

"Frozen or Fresh?"

"Frozen."

"Really? That's so great!" I've had numerous conversations with strangers that included the words "cervical mucus."

Not only the incidence of twins, but also the incidence of mothers who have their first child at over the age of thirty-five continues to rise. These days, one in seven first children are born to women over thirty-five, and the number of women past forty having children has more than doubled in the last ten years.

What this means in practical terms (and by "practical," I mean "terms that will make you buy this book") is that there are an awful lot of women out there with tidy houses and tidy husbands and child-substitute pets with names like Timothy who now find themselves drowning in Similac: women who would no more discuss excretory functions than volunteer for a tax audit, yet are suddenly willing and able to write a doctoral dissertation on poo. Women, in short, like me: Geezers with Children.

Hillary Clinton was dead right when she said "it takes a village" to raise a child; grandparents, she noted, play a crucial role in the lives of young ones. The problem for older mothers is that often our village is, not to put too fine a point on it, dead—or at best too frail to participate in child rearing. Our husbands too are often older. Many have been down this road before with first families and are less than overjoyed at the prospect of spit-ups and 3 A.M. feedings. And baby-friendly pals are not always at hand. If we managed to extend our own childhoods into our late thirties and forties, as many of us have, we've accumulated a circle of child-free friends who are as terrified by All Things Baby as we were until we crossed the Great Divide.

(Every woman who's had a baby later in life recognizes her own personal moment of crossing. For me it was the day my sons were two months old, and I was taking a break, sitting by myself in a restaurant. A man at a nearby table burped softly and without thinking I shouted, "Good job!")

Fortunately, many older mothers have money. So we can often buy our village, in the form of nurses, nannies, and other child-care providers. During the first three months of my sons' lives, my shell-shocked husband (who was sixty-six—not the ideal age for child rearing unless you're Tony Randall) virtually moved out of the house and I shacked up with a Jamaican woman named Yvonne. She knew everything about babies and had me thoroughly cowed. On the plus side, she kept my children very clean. I think she had them Scotchgarded.

I haven't even mentioned the universal problem of motherhood that nevertheless hits older mothers hardest: sleep deprivation. If you think a twenty-five-year-old is exhausted after a few nights of bad to no sleep, try talking to a forty-year-old. My most common response to the question "How are you?" was *"What do you mean by that?"*

Then, of course, there's the question of what late motherhood does to a marriage. When you've become accustomed over the years to complete spontaneity, babies are a gonglike wake-up call. I still remember the evening when Henry and Gus were about four months old and my husband and I decided to see a movie. We had our coats on and were headed out the door when we stopped. Oh. What do we do with *them?*

One day, as I was looking at the Hanna Andersson catalogue—cursing the small print and all the mothers whose eyesight was still good enough to read it—I decided I wanted to write an honest account of what new motherhood is like when you're a woman past that first bloom of youth—or, as a friend's dinosaur-obsessed seven-year-old called it, a momasaurus.

I started with the idea that I would chronicle the first year of life, but I discovered that for much of the first year, a child is pretty much like a messy, high-maintenance plant. So eventually I figured, OK, the diary will end when my boys take their first steps. I figured this would be twelve, thirteen months tops. That took me to eighteen and a half months, since one of my sons inherited his mother's stunning athleticism. And then?

When I was a kid learning to knit, I knit myself a belt that was twenty-two feet long because nobody told me how to tie off the ends. Unfortunately, I'm not much better at tying off the ends now.

So this is an account of the first twenty months of my sons' lives. The book ends, quite logically, when my editors at Miramax began to shout at me.

THE FIRST THING I THOUGHT when I saw my sons was, "I wonder if they'd look less like space aliens if I penciled in their eyebrows."

The second thing I thought was "They're both alive."

Which was by no means a foregone conclusion.

But I'm getting ahead of myself, by about seven years. In 1994 I started out as a youngish woman who inexplicably couldn't have a baby. If you keep doing fertility treatments long enough, however, you end up being a woman who can't have a baby for a very good reason: you're old. The phrase most often used by specialists is "advanced maternal age." But I appreciated the nurse at one fertility clinic who called it as she saw it: we were the "geriatric mothers."

Until this point I'd had little experience with disappointment. It's not just that my life had been blessed, though it had (my parents were still alive, I had work I loved, my husband annoyed me only fifty percent of the time). No, the real reason I never got disappointed was that I was the queen of low expectations. A close friend gossips about me behind my back. Eh, what can you do? People talk about each other; it's human nature. My husband, John, refuses to go away with me, after I'd been looking forward to a vacation for months. Well, I knew he was moody when I married him; why should I expect him to change? Of course, the pleasant flip side of low expectations is that you're always a little shocked when something goes right. You mean to say the plane is leaving on time and I might make it home before the polar ice caps melt? *Whoo!* If you never want anything too badly, you'll never be disappointed: that's always been my motto.

So when disappointment hit, I wasn't prepared. *What do you mean I can't get pregnant?* Just look at me! I remembered years ago going on a blind date with a man from India; when we met he looked at me appraisingly, eyed my hips, and said, "I can see you'll bear many children easily." Hey, he meant it as a compliment.

When you start confessing to friends that you can't get pregnant, everyone has a surefire solution. Acupuncture! Herbal teas! Cruises! So many people suggested John and I sail to the Bahamas that I began to wonder if cruises weren't actually a form of time travel, by which I would end up with the eggs of an eighteen-year-old.

My own thoughts turned toward moving to a trailer park and drinking. Have you ever heard of anyone who lives in a trailer park having problems getting pregnant? Furthermore, most of these people seemed to conceive after a night of tequila shots. I tried this method. Many times. Had I gotten pregnant during those lost weekends, I imagine the child would have been born with a slice of lime in the corner of her mouth.

When you first decide to make a baby, you can't believe your luck: finally, you and this person you love enough to share a gene pool with can do what nature intended without pills, latex, foams, or goo! It's beautiful. It's almost sacred. But during those years of trying to conceive (or, as it's abbreviated on all the Internet infertility support groups, TTC), one's attitude toward sex evolves in a fairly predictable pattern. It goes something like this:

Fucking
Making love
Having sex
Mating
Performing a science experiment

At the end, for many of us, that's exactly what it is: a science experiment. And a pricey one too. Insurance pays for only some of the diagnostic tests and virtually none of the treatments; a one-month round of in vitro fertilization costs ten to twelve thousand dollars. The only other medical field similarly shunned by insurance companies is plastic surgery. It seems that in some way the two are perceived as morally equivalent—medical treatments demanded by vain women obsessed by their DNA, attempting to get their hands on what nature has denied them. Boob jobs and babies, both life's frills. Or, as I heard so frequently about infertility, *"Hey, it's not cancer."*

I began keeping records of the Baby Quest on July 25, 1995, and continued, when I wasn't paralyzed by sadness, for the next six years. Endless tests were repeated; endless doctors were visited; endless promises made. Here are some sample entries:

July 25, 1995

I'm hoping this will be the world's shortest infertility journal. Today I'm virtually positive I'm not pregnant: I'm weepy, depressed, distracted—all those charming PMS signs. My friend Maria said to me today, "It sounds as if you're upset not about not having a baby, but about having a goal you can't attain." She has a point. But that's because I can't think that far ahead. I can't get dewy-eyed about a person I don't know.

John has been so sweet, so cooperative, but his melancholy nature is no help at a time like this. "Well, if you can't have children, we can travel," he says. I want to shout, "You know what? I've been meaning to tell you this for years: I don't really *like* to travel! I don't even like to watch the Discovery Channel!"

September 2, 1995

John wakes me up in the middle of the night. Through my stupor I think, "I still love to look at you." He's a bull of a man, compact, hairy, and powerful. Growing up in the north of England, he used to pick up cars for a free pint; even now he can bench-press 250 pounds. With his barrel chest, bandy legs, enormous head, and curtain of white hair falling over oyster gray eyes, he looks like a caricature of an opera singer, which is exactly what he was. A perfectionist, he retired the day he decided his voice wasn't what it used to be. No one could talk him out of it.

"I'm really too old to do this," he says.

"Shut up," I say.

"I told you when we got married, if you wanted a child you had to have one right away. Now I'm over sixty and—"

"Warren Beatty," I begin tiredly. "Anthony Quinn. Clint Eastwood. Norman Lear."

"Do you notice that one thing they all have in common? *Money.*"

"Don't worry. We'll stop at one. I promise."

He sighs. "I never liked children even when I was a child."

"Me neither. Go to sleep."

November 15, 1995
Let the testing begin. Instructions for men:

HOW TO COLLECT A SEMEN SPECIMEN

Wake up horny. Talk about how much you want to do it.
Realize you can't do it, as "it" needs to go into a cup.
Fight to remember how much you wanted to do it only
minutes earlier.

Go into the bathroom and wash your genitals thoroughly
with Hibiclens, an antiseptic/antimicrobial skin
cleanser that looks like melted cherry lollipop. Then
wash your hands. Then wipe them on towel. Realize
towel is probably crawling with microbes, and start
the whole process again.

Come out of the bathroom and realize your wife can't
touch you until *she* washes with Hibiclens. She darts
into the bathroom to wash. You touch yourself gin-
gerly, wondering if you're ever going to have a hard-
on, ever again.

Your wife comes out of the bathroom, holding up her
hands like a surgeon. She's scrubbed them raw. Note
for later: Remind her she's been watching too many
episodes of *ER.* She lies down next to you and you
begin to kiss. You can't touch her for fear of bacteria,

and besides, she's fully dressed. She must be, because if you ever actually do accomplish your mission, she's got to race up to the lab, which is way uptown, in order to deliver your specimen. Time is of the essence: the fresher the stuff is, the better. Of course you could simply go to the lab and produce your specimen there, in a nice clean bathroom supplied with *Playboys* and *Penthouses*. But the chances of your becoming aroused under those circumstances are approximately equal to what the Bills have of winning the Super Bowl.

Try to concentrate. Concentrate more. Be totally impotent for the first time in your life. Try not to fixate on the impending divorce when your wife giggles.

Keep trying. Give up. Go into the bathroom. Think of yourself as a piñata which will burst forth with treats, if only you swing the bat hard enough. Start swinging.

Emerge from the bathroom, disgusted but triumphant. Call what you've just done "a soul-destroying experience." Notice that your wife is ignoring you. She kisses you on the cheek and bolts for the door, having buried plastic cup deep in her cleavage to keep it warm. Shout after her: "Tell the guys at the lab there isn't as much in there as I usually produce." Realize that, as if on cue, your next-door neighbor is leaving his apartment to go to work.

In all those dramatic dashes uptown, I usually could not control my urge to freak out the cab driver. "The hospital, please, and step on it! My semen only has an hour to live!" Of course *semen* probably means something like "roast potato" in Urdu, so I didn't always get the reaction I wanted.

November 20, 1995

The test on Day 3 of my menstrual cycle shows that the level of FSH in my blood is low. This is good; it means my body is not having to work hard to pump out the necessary hormone that triggers ovulation. John's sperm count is OK, his motility is so-so: on the fertility highway, he's doing 40 in a 60 mph zone. Still, that should be enough to get us where we want to go. Should be, but hasn't. Of course, it's taken me one year to figure out that the time I was absolutely positive I was ovulating turns out to be four days short of the time I actually was. I've been spending thirty dollars a month on five of those little ovulation-tester sticks, and when the little line in the big window didn't turn blue at the right time, I'd think, "Well, I'm one of the one percent of people for whom these sticks don't work." Then someone finally urged me to keep testing, and lo, on the eighteenth day, the stick turned blue—just about the time that John and I were so exhausted from the previous days' sperm injections, as we so romantically called them, that we gave ourselves a few days of rest. Is it

possible I could have missed that window of opportunity for
one solid year?

Given how many things can get botched along the way,
it's astounding anyone gets born at all.

November 30, 1995

Now John and I are looking at the distinct possibility that
we are allergic to each other. Tomorrow we go for sperm
antibody testing. A couple of days ago, a perky child in a lab
coat—I believe she stole the coat from a real doctor—
harvested some of my cervical mucus on the day I had my
LH surge, a tidal wave of hormone which induces ovulation.
She injected it into a tube and instructed me to freeze it. So
now I've got bodily secretions hidden behind a can of
Minute Maid orange juice. The next day, after five days of
abstinence during which John and I fought over things like
who forgot to buy a new carrot scraper, we did *it* and went
in the following morning to see how John's sperm were
faring inside me. It was pretty much Hiroshima in there. So
tomorrow John and I and our secretions have a date with a
man who's going to determine if my body is looking at my
husband's sperm as tiny foreign invaders storming the
Normandy that is my uterus.

I started to explain to John—who was drawing all sorts of
dire conclusions about our relationship because of our possible

9

bodily incompatibility—that if I'm allergic to his sperm, I'm probably allergic to *all* sperm, not just his; if any semen had ever somehow seeped into my circulatory system, antibodies to it could have built up over time. That, of course, raised the appalling possibility that at some point in the distant past I had had more than a passing acquaintance with semen that was not his. John didn't talk to me for the rest of the day.

February 16, 1996

The last phase in John's testing: the sperm penetration test or, as I think of it, the date with the hamster. First hamsters are superovulated, and then the man's sperm is tested to see if it can break through the egg wall. John and I went through the usual jokes: Shouldn't he be buying the hamster dinner first? Bringing it flowers, maybe a Habitrail? etc. When I went to the lab office, I was surprised to discover that the technician was not standing there, a hamster in tow. The sperm is put into some sort of solution that keeps it viable for a few days (why can't they do that inside me?) and sent off to a nearby lab where the hamster is—well, the truth is I don't want to know what they do to the hamster. Is it sacrificed? Or is it merely subject to incredible mood swings, the result of being put on fertility drugs? Maybe scores of hamsters are sitting in labs, weeping and shredding boxes of Kleenex right now.

March 16, 1996

My blood is tested for progesterone levels. The idea here is to see if I've got the appropriate amount of progesterone to sustain a pregnancy, should one occur.

The first day of these visits is bitterly cold; I wear a down jacket that makes me look like a Macy's Thanksgiving Day float but helps me withstand all temperatures. As I put the coat on after the blood test, the zipper, as usual, gets stuck. I try to force it, hop about, step out of the coat, curse under my breath. After about ten minutes of this, I notice an elderly couple in the waiting room staring at me intently. The woman's lips are parted in anticipation, her eyes bright. Finally she nudges her husband and whispers in his ear. This is his cue.

"Excuse me, Miss. My wife is an expert with zippers. Mind if she gives it a try?"

Gladly I hand over my coat, and she works on the zipper with a zeal and dexterity that's rather surprising, considering that this blood collection station doubles as a waiting room for people with joint diseases. Her fingers are gnarled and eager. In less than a minute, without ripping the fabric wedged into the zipper, she fixes the problem and smiles triumphantly.

Her husband explains. "This is how Millie and I met. I was skiing, and my zipper got stuck. This cute redhead came over and offered to fix it, and she did. I figured any girl who was that handy was the girl I had to marry. And so I did. That was fifty years ago today." They smile at each other shyly.

I make myself leave before I ask them whether they had children.

April 1996
Vaginal cultures came back negative. Progesterone levels are fine. Second day of my period. What the hell is my problem?

May 4, 1996
There's an old saying a doctor once told me: If you think you're healthy, you simply haven't had enough tests yet.

Tomorrow I'm going in for a laparoscopy, which will determine if there's anything structurally wrong with my reproductive organs. The doc will shoot dye through my fallopian tubes, get rid of a small polyp, zap any endometriosis he might find with a laser—in short, give me a new, improved reproductive system.

May 6, 1996
The operation itself was nothing, but as usual when I woke up, I was reeling with nausea. This was supposed to be day surgery. I had my operation at 8 A.M., and I was still

incapable of getting up and out of there by 9 P.M. I was the last person left in the recovery room.

After plying me with Compazine and other quasi-placebos, the nurse finally admitted that they were reluctant to give me the most powerful drug in their arsenal, Zofran, because it was expensive. "Probably not as expensive," I pointed out, "as keeping this recovery room open on a Friday night till two in the morning." I got the drug and left at 10:00 P.M.

Unfortunately, nothing is seriously wrong. Rather than being the L.A. freeway at rush hour I imagined, my tubes are open wide. Just a few polyps in utero, nothing that would have prevented me from getting pregnant.

TWO VIVID POST-OP DREAMS:

1. I am on a beach, worried because I don't have sunblock. I squint into the sun and notice pairs of ostriches in Day-Glo colors flying by at tremendous speeds. They are dive-bombing, two by two, into the sea. Enormous diving fluffballs of the most fantastic colors. Damn, drugs are good.

2. I am in a postapocalyptic world where boulders the size of apartment buildings are raining down on Earth. If I keep looking up and see them in time, I can dodge them. One has grazed my arm, but I survive. I am

holding a flute made of stone—like one of those wooden Peruvian instruments—and I very much want to play. But playing means looking down, and if I look down, I'll probably be crushed. Almost everyone I know has removed their gaze from the sky, and they've been crushed. Almost everyone I know is gone. Is it worth it to keep looking up and play no music?

May 20, 1996

I am going to try and take the next few months and relax, see if nature will take its course. I'm probably the least nurturing person in existence. I don't think I could get a Chia Pet to grow.

July 14, 1996

As it becomes increasingly obvious I'm going to get my period, John says, "Well, the moral of this story is, *Never wait too long when you want something.*" At which point I become hysterical, pointing out, quite rightly, that if I wanted to feel horrible and filled with remorse, I could do that very well without his help, thank you very much.

Perhaps the worst PMS I've ever had.

July 20, 1996

The hell with nature. Nature has let me down. Let's see
what science has to offer.

August 1, 1996

Met with Mark Sauer, the director of Columbia
Presbyterian's infertility program. Relaxed, genial, looks
remarkably like Bill Murray—thought he might give me
noogies. Fortunately, he didn't laugh too hard when I
produced my husband's meticulous records of my cycles
recorded over the last two years. John is the Felix Unger of
menstruation.

Dr. Sauer has four children himself—two boys, two girls—
and at one point he started complaining to me good-naturedly
about them. Then, awkwardly, he stopped, which made me
feel even more like an object of pity than I already do.

I explained how frightened I am of taking fertility drugs,
terrified of shots, terrified of getting ovarian cancer from the
drugs, terrified I'd have more than one child. I asked him
what he would do if his sister were to come to him with this
problem, and he looked a little pale. "Actually, my sister
almost did come to me with this problem. She had an ectopic
pregnancy, lost one of her tubes, and for a while it looked
like I'd have to do IVF on her," he said. "It was just terrible.

It was like, I knew I'd have my mother calling me every day and saying, 'Have you gotten your sister pregnant yet?'"

Until a few months ago Sauer had been known mainly as a researcher; he just came here from USC. As we were talking, he received a phone call. "Oh, you got eighteen eggs from her. Great. I'll talk to you later." Some time passed. Then another call. "All the sperm is dead? You're kidding. Well, I don't want her to have gone through all this for nothing. Find some other sperm. I don't care where you get it."

For the next ten minutes, everything else Dr. Sauer said was white noise. *"Find some other sperm. I don't care where you get it"*: these are not welcome words to a person considering insemination. Finally I had the nerve to pipe up, "Um, when you said 'find some other sperm,' what exactly did you mean?" He replied, "Well, we could just get another batch somewhere. We'll order it in."

There was a pause, as I contemplated bolting from the room. "Oh, I'm sorry," he said. "Maybe you didn't understand. I'm talking about *monkeys.* We're doing research on some new drugs and..."

Suddenly I found I could breathe again.

November 7, 1996
Beginning of Perganol shots. All those years John spent
playing darts in pubs have paid off: shots in butt don't hurt
at all. What was I so scared of?

November 11, 1996
So now I am on Day 11 of my normal cycle, but I may be on
Day 4 of my drug cycle. I'm really not sure. The drugs give
the body a kind of hormonal jet lag: one doesn't know where
one is in the scheme of things, or why. But at any rate, I'm
proud of my ability to do this thing I swore I couldn't do.
John takes care of the huge Perganol needles in my bottom;
I do the tiny Lupron shots (the drug that shuts down my
natural cycle) in the stomach. Every time I jab myself—
right side, then left, then right—I'm humming Helen
Reddy: "I am woman, hear me roar." I've become a
connoisseur of pain too. The sides are less painful than the
middle; the closer one gets to the belly button, the more
nerves in the area; hence, stay away.

John prepares the needles, though, because for all my
bravery I am not brave enough to risk injecting myself with
air bubbles. I trust John to know what an air bubble is and to
avoid it. (Of course, now he has the perfect alibi for my death:
"Doc, I was injecting her, and *I just missed that one bubble.*")

November 21, 1996

Dirty Debutantes: That was the name of the video John and I were handed this morning. It wasn't just the tape that was fun, it was the fact that they put it in a briefcase and that you have to march down a very long hall to a room with a VCR. Something about that march... "Well, good-bye, honey, I'm off to a day of hard work and masturbation!" In the dingy room there was a fold-out futon bed with sheets that apparently hadn't been changed, a tiny TV with VCR, and a sink and toilet behind a partition. The trash next to the toilet hadn't been emptied. Perhaps, we told each other hopefully, the hospital staff had been playing with the design theme "cheesy motel," the better to induce fantasies of pillow-lipped hookers and flat-assed cowboys. With some difficulty we folded out the futon couch into a bed, lay down, and concentrated. "I almost thought it wasn't going to work," John said later, but work it did, in less than five minutes. As we walked back down that long, long hall with the specimen in my pocket, John swung the briefcase jauntily.

Insemination was quick and virtually painless. After all the dead and freak sperm were cleared away, we were left with about seven million. Shot right up in my uterus—how tough could it be for them to get where they needed to go? I visualized sperm being whisked along in those little airplane terminal go-carts, humming a cheerful tune as they headed toward a desired destination. They were all wearing matching little white belts and shoes.

Afterward, John came in and held my hand as we glanced around the tiny, windowless pink room, noting the cheap Manet prints of ladies at the seashore and thinking, quietly, "Thank God there is this."

November 25, 1996
John and I argue over whether, if I get pregnant, we should donate his frozen sperm to some deserving person. I take the William F. Buckleyesque position: it's the duty of the reasonably intelligent and nice to spread their seed. John, Mr. Glass Half Empty, argues how awful it would be if a nice intelligent child got trapped in a family of morons. Perhaps we put a little too much faith in genetics.

And perhaps we need to get over ourselves.

December 5, 1996
Failure.

December 6, 1996
Don't get out of the house.

December 7, 1996
Don't get out of the house.

December 8, 1996
Don't get out of bed.

December 9, 1996
Got a grip. Sort of. Made an appointment with a psychic. But not just any psychic. She's the psychic for Goldie Hawn and Demi Moore. How bad could their lives be, that they need this lady?

Sobbed in the subway over a picture of a baby gorilla advertising the Bronx Zoo.

December 19, 1996
So Goldie Hawn's psychic tells me she sees me with a son, Samuel, who will be either born or conceived in March— exactly what year is not clear. "He will be annoying as a small child, very playful, and he'll never stop talking," she says. "But that's OK, because later when he's a teenager the two of you will be great friends. He wants to be a lawyer or a news reporter, he's not sure which. But he'll make money." Thank God someone will.

February 20, 1997
On Valentine's Day John cheerfully admitted to me that sex had become totally unconnected to pleasure for him. Thanks for sharing! Here I was, doing everything in my power to

compartmentalize this situation—OK, sex for a few days of the month was rather clinical, but hey, the rest of the time, let's party! I thought I was doing such a good job, and meanwhile my husband is looking at me with about the same degree of pleasure as Sisyphus looks at a rock.

I was hurt hurt hurt and can't let it go. I bring it up subtly at every opportunity. *"Honey, can you please pass the salt—unless that feels like too much of an effort for you."* So now he feels like he's going to make love to me *a lot,* to prove what a goddess I am. As if this whole situation weren't unpleasant enough, now I know I'm making my husband fake it.

February 21, 1997
Today I looked at my sweaty, twenty-year-old Italian butcher and thought, *"I bet it would work with him."*

March, April, May 1997
Failure and herbs and more failure. I loved going to the herbalist, I really did. All those little drawers full of mud and twigs that promised to add up to a baby. I swallowed pills I eventually found out contained human placenta, illegally imported from China. (*"You no tell nobody, OK?"*) I loved the way she held my wrist, writing down mysterious numbers and assuring me that babies would be "no problem."

They were a problem.

June 1, 1997

Got hypnotized, perhaps a little too well. All I can remember is being unable to put hands to my face to brush the tears away. I was floating, and the floating was awful because I was unconnected from everything and everyone.

June 16, 1997

One more round of insemination before ramping up to IVF—this time, with Cecilia Schmidt Sarosi. She and her husband, Dr. Peter Sarosi, have six children between them; her last son she had naturally at forty-five, after being operated on for breast cancer. This gives me hope.

Today, as I was splayed out in the examining room, I heard a slightly panicked nurse yelling at a patient over the phone: "No, no! You don't *swallow* it! If it's digested, it's useless! What did you think all those needles were for? *Yes,* it makes a difference!"

You are supposed to mix the little ampules of powdered hormone with sterile water, then inject the stuff into your stomach. But apparently this patient decided it would be just as effective, and considerably less painful, to simply swallow the powder, then wash it down with the sterile water. She had swallowed a thousand dollars' worth of Fertinex before the nurse set her straight.

June 20, 1997

Another hypnosis session, this time more successful. "You have a right to be pregnant," Stephanie tells me. "You don't have to be perfect, you can still be ambivalent, but you also have the right to be pregnant." Silly maybe, but those were soothing words and soothing thoughts.

She told me to visualize myself as a lush garden.

July 3, 1997

I am not a lush garden. My uterus is marble, smooth, and cool. Nothing can find purchase there.

July 6, 1997

Period started yesterday. My poor mother wants to talk to me about all this, and I don't want to talk back. We are a feedback loop, a Möbius ring of sorrow, because of course she had the same problem having me. "I used to want to kill women who told me, 'Oh, I got drunk at a party one night, and that's how it happened,'" she said. Then she talks to me about the next-door neighbor who got a puppy. "I think she just wanted another baby. That dog is in her arms all the time."

In her arms. How many people tell me that's how you know you want a baby: that sense of needing to hold something tiny and helpless. I don't have that feeling at all. I was thinking last night that if John got horribly sick, I could take care of him in the most intimate way. He could puke and be incontinent, and I wouldn't be bothered at all, or rather, I'd be miserable, but only for his shame and indignity. I expect I would have that feeling for a child, but I certainly don't feel it now. Nothing like it. I'm mindful of the Oscar Wilde line "Be careful what you wish for."

Yet here I sit on Sunday morning, wrung out, eyes swollen, hoping for grace that never comes.

DURING THE NEXT TWO YEARS I went through three rounds of in vitro fertilization. Here eggs are removed from the body, fertilized in a petri dish, and the resulting embryos are poured back in. Each time I did a round of IVF, I got pregnant. Each time, I planned how I would decorate the kid's dorm at Princeton. Each time, I had a miscarriage. After the first miscarriage there was this journal entry:

At least I had the satisfaction of learning that the miscarriage happened because two sperm mistakenly fertilized one egg, causing a genetic mishmash. This was good, because I could then turn around and blame John. Everything about him is so . . . overzealous.

And after the second there was this:

May 4, 1998

For the two hundredth time yesterday my mother hesitatingly mentioned the word *adoption.* Adoption. Certain friends, too, mention it in every conversation. Why don't you adopt? You'll be saving some child who needs a home...you'll be helping...you'll be doing...you'll be caring...

People mean well, but I hear in that question the silent reproof: *Why are you so selfish?* I want to say, Let me tell you. I don't adopt because if you look at the statistics, the number of self-reported unhappy adoptees is huge. I don't adopt because even the happy adoptees I know have waited until their parents were dead to find their biological parents; the adoptive parents are rarely enough. I don't adopt because you can't turn on the television set without seeing people's lives torn apart by an irreparably damaged child who just "needed loving to straighten out." I don't adopt because I'm a biological determinist. I don't adopt because my genes are enough of a crapshoot, never mind anyone else's. I don't adopt because my husband is old and I want him with me forever, so I'm hoping to get *my husband swaddled in a blanket.*

And I don't adopt because I don't know what my capacity for love is. Are you satisfied now?

SOMETIMES, IN A PERVERSE ATTEMPT to make myself feel better, I'd go to an infertility support group board on the Internet to find people who were even worse off than I was:

> *I have had three miscarriages and two tubal pregnancies. I am divorced, no partner to even have a child with now, and my doctor says it doesn't look good with only one tube and my previous history.*

> *I spent my Sunday in the ER....They did an internal exam and then they pulled my baby out of my cervix. I stated that I wanted to see it...I haven't cried yet.*

> *Today was the EDD (estimated due date) of my twin babies and it hit me hard. I was supposed to have newborn babies for this Christmas. It just hurts.*

Everyone tried to be kind, even when they weren't. "Don't worry; you got pregnant, you'll be able to get pregnant again." This observation was a little wearing by the third miscarriage. "You need to relax." Yes, why don't *you* try to relax when you're spending fifteen thousand dollars you can't afford to be pumped so full of progesterone you'd like to gnaw your own leg off? My personal favorite: "Well, now you have three angels up in Heaven." Hello, I'm not all that interested in creating little helpers for the Almighty! I'd be much happier to have one small devil down here.

After the third miscarriage, I went to the animal shelter in East Hampton and adopted the most beautiful, stupid dog I could find. Before I decided on Monty, I gave him the dog intelligence test. First wave a ball in front of dog and watch him go berserk with joy. Then take ball and ostentatiously hide it under a newspaper. A dog with two brain cells to rub together will look at you, look at the newspaper, and immediately start nosing for the ball. Monty looked at me, looked all around, then stared at me in wonder: *"How did you manage to make that ball disappear? You are a practitioner of the black arts! I shall worship you!"* Intelligence in dogs is overrated, I feel. Who wants a dog that can figure out how to use a can opener?

Monty had been abandoned by a woman who had three children under the age of five. She got him as a puppy, thinking the kids and the golden retriever would make a lovely picture at Christmas. But the puppy proved too needy. Hope her kids never prove too needy, I thought churlishly, as Monty drenched me with saliva on the car ride home.

Later that evening John, who loves dogs, was nevertheless not overjoyed to be greeted by a hundred-pound golden retriever with three tennis balls in his mouth. "Doesn't he look like Harrison Ford?" I said, pointing out the triangular cast of the eyes and the noble firm jaw.

"This isn't funny," John said, as Monty dropped the slimy tennis balls in his lap, wagging furiously. "You don't make time in your life for a cactus, never mind *this.*" Monty wedged his knobby skull between John's knees. "You're a sewer of a dog," John murmured resignedly, as he skritched his ears for fifteen minutes.

Like the character in literature John most closely resembles, Uncle Matthew in the Nancy Mitford novels, it is his tragic fate to be a magnet for the pets and children he shuns. Indeed when thinking of my husband I've often had reason to think of Uncle Matthew and the description of him by Mitford's alter ego, Fanny, in *Love in a Cold Climate*: "Much as we feared, much as we disapproved of, passionately as we sometimes hated Uncle Matthew, he still remained for us a sort of criterion of English manhood. There seemed something not quite right about a man who greatly differed from him."

John left early that evening to go home. As it happens John *could* leave, because he had another home to go to. After eight years of marriage we still didn't live together. Marriage is one thing, but cohabitation? There are some things people shouldn't rush into.

Before I met John, this was the décor of my 750-square-foot apartment: On the first floor was a stamp-sized kitchen and dining room with no table, and an adjacent bedroom with a futon on the floor and a desk for work. Walk up seven steps to the elevated living room, and you would find a coffee table of a vaguely Southwestern style, a chair from my parents' basement, and on some days a Tokay gecko lounging on the ceiling. I'd bought the gecko to keep away roaches and also as a further extension of my nascent Southwestern theme. But for some reason I inhabited the only apartment in New York City without a bustling roach population. So to feed the Tokay I had to buy crickets and let them loose, making my apartment sound on some nights like Walton's Mountain. Apparently at one point I wasn't fast enough in replenishing the cricket supply, and the gecko disappeared. I imagine it's now eight feet long, albino, and living behind my walls.

At any rate, my only other furnishings at the time were a television and several pots and pans, stored in the oven, which hadn't been turned on since I had moved in two years earlier. I had Scotch-taped photographs of Chip Simon dogs on the walls and hung a lithograph of Andy Warhol's *Electric Chair* my mother had inexplicably and somewhat alarmingly given me for my twenty-first birthday.

John has a deeply domestic bent, or at least what I consider domestic, meaning he told me I had to buy furniture. But even with the furniture John couldn't stand to live with me. I can't say I blame him. John is a man who can't sleep if he knows his shoes are not lined up in the closet. I don't understand why shoes—or for that matter, anything else—

should be lined up in a closet if you're just going to put them on the next day.

There was yet another reason for our keeping separate apartments. Early on we decided that commingling finances wasn't such a great idea, since I am not terribly cautious in this regard and John is—what's the word I'm looking for here?—cheap. With himself, more than with anyone else. The Turnbull & Asser shirts I've bought him over the years lie pristine and untouched in his drawers; he prefers to scavenge old clothing from the incinerator room in my apartment building. "Hey, I remember those pants!" is a common greeting to John from our neighbors.

In my moments of displeasure I remind myself that he is retired and lives off his investments. And he will give of his time and energy and concern a thousand times more than I, who'd rather write a check. But money?

I hate people who buy into cultural stereotypes.

Did I mention John's originally from Scotland?

For the first years after we married and continued to live separately we thought we were chic. We'd announce our living arrangements to anyone who'd listen. "Very Woody and Mia!" we used to say. Then Soon-Yi came along, and we sort of shut up.

But to return to my original point: having a dog in the city was not on my husband's to-do list. He saw the expense—I was not one to stint on twenty-dollar-an-hour walkers, hundred-dollar groomers, and fifteen-dollar buckets of dried chicken liver treats—and he saw the inconvenience. He was also quick to point out that in my hormone-addled state I shouldn't be making a decision about a living creature that required hours of attention and exercise a day.

I was very contrite and apologized profusely. At least, that's what I remember. John remembers the conversation differently. "Drop dead," I reportedly said.

I've always believed dogs are not child substitutes. If anything, children are dog substitutes. Some days I still feel that way.

Still.

ACCORDING TO AN ARTICLE published about ten years ago in the *New England Journal of Medicine,* a group of women who'd had a baby through IVF were asked how many times they tried. Forty-four percent said once, about forty percent said twice, ten percent said three times, and four percent said four times. If it didn't work the first three times, it wasn't very likely to work thereafter.

I was thirty-eight and a three-time loser. My chances of success had dwindled precipitously. What was the point of doing anything more? After the third miscarriage, there was this journal entry:

So I'm to get through life without knowing this one thing, this love. So what? Does the universe care about one less person? No; the universe rejoices. We are crushing this planet anyway, we humans. I am doing the planet a favor.

I grieved for a year. Then I decided I didn't owe the planet any favors.

BE CAREFUL WHAT YOU WISH FOR. In January 2000 I switched clinics, this time to NYU Hospital. The success rate of their infertility program is one of the highest in the country—about thirty percent live births per cycle for women in my age range—and NYU did not boost its success rates, like many clinics do, by turning away the hardest cases.

"You have a really interestingly shaped cervix," said Jamie Grifo, the clinic's director, before doing something down there that left me clinging to the ceiling by my fingernails. "Um, remind me to give you a Valium IV when we do the egg retrieval," he added.

Jamie Grifo is a compact, handsome man with salt-and-pepper hair, deep-set black eyes, and the ashen pallor of someone who spends too much time under artificial light. He is a dead ringer for Al Pacino, and the few times we met he was always doing a slow burn about something. I began to think of him not so much as a fertility doctor as Michael Corleone after finding out about Fredo.

Part of his fury, I eventually discovered, stemmed from problems with research outside the clinic. The FDA had objected to some of his research, which involved transferring the DNA of an older woman with bad eggs into the healthy, nutrient-rich egg of a young woman whose own DNA has been removed. In the conservative political climate of the moment, the procedure seemed too close to cloning for the agency's tastes, although it was in truth nothing of the sort. I tsk-tsked the FDA's decision, and once he realized he had a sympathetic audience, he went off on a tear. Very endearing, if a little mad scientist.

I suspect most of his anger stemmed from his inability to get it right one hundred percent of the time. The pregnancy odds weren't in his favor. If he made thirty-five percent of his patients ecstatic, that still meant there were sixty-five percent who were crushed. Grifo was by nature a perfectionist, and these odds, even though they were among the best anywhere, made him a testy guy. When I expressed a faint hope that maybe this cycle would work despite my previous failures, he promised nothing, offering only a grim "I will do my best."

He did.

February 12, 2001

Almost didn't make it to the doctor's in time. I'd been interviewing Barbara Walters; she was doing an ABC Special on adoption, and we were talking about her adopted daughter. The interview was running late. *"Sorry, gotta run, need to be fertilized!"*: It just didn't seem like the time or place, though I'm quite sure she would have understood and even cheered me on.

Still woozy from the Valium drip. Fifteen eggs, nine fertilized, but a mere three made it healthily to Day 5; these are the contenders. They were thrown in today. Immediately beforehand I was told I had an "embryo upgrade." As it turns out, this means the cell balls were looking better than they had been looking early that morning. But in my stupor I had an idea that maybe it was like an upgrade of seats on an airplane; maybe they were just giving me *better ones.* I'd just read something about how many frozen embryos are left over from people's IVF procedures, and I figured maybe the winner of the Booker Prize or the chairman of MIT's physics department had just been here and left some extras.

I remember nothing. But a nurse told me later that I had instructed Dr. Grifo to add any extra embryos he had lying around if they came from nice, intelligent people; I had said that ignorance is bliss and what you don't know doesn't hurt you and I would never, ever sue.

February 14, 2001
Last night I dreamt that the embryologist at NYU had been replaced by Martha Stewart. I was on the table, my legs in stirrups, and Martha informed me that although my zygotes were already extremely attractive, the best way to ensure that they adhere to the walls of the uterus was *this*—and she held up her glue gun. Then I woke up.

February 20, 2001
Two pink lines. Yeah, so what? Been here before. Three times. And where has it gotten me? Still, at 6 A.M. I sob with relief and climb back into bed. I put my arm around John, who holds my hand and says nothing.

February 22, 2001
HCG [Human Chorionic Gonadotropin, a hormone secreted by an embryo, indicating the existence of a pregnancy] reading 249. It's never been that high.

February 24, 2001
HCG 519. It's more than doubled in two days. I was queasy a week ago. Now I am almost incapacitated with nausea.

The nurse tells me these readings are consistent with the implantation of two embryos. I know this is impossible, because it would be horrible and not at all what I planned. I shake off the thought. Anyway, I can barely think about getting through another day, never mind what will happen eight months from now.

March 12, 2001

In the velvet darkness of the ultrasound room Dr. Grifo harpoons me with the vagin-o-gram. He takes a few measurements, squints at the screen. He's a little bored and probably hungry; it's right before lunchtime. "Two sacs," he says perfunctorily. "Congratulations."

Two. *Two?*

In the ensuing silence, there's a whooshing sound. Is it their hearts? Or mine?

"I hate the name Jamie," I say. "But what's your middle name? In case either one is a boy?"

"Anthony," he says softly. It's the first time I've ever seen him smile.

WHEN A WOMAN DISCOVERS she's having twins, two thoughts immediately leap to mind:

1. Oh my God, they're going to look so adorable in matching outfits!
2. Oh my God, they're going to be speaking to each other in some creepy second language.

These, at least, were *my* two thoughts (closely followed by "If I stay in New York City and have to send them to private school, that's $40,000 a year after taxes..."). I had no desire to have twins. As a happy only child, I thought the ideal family consisted of a mother, father, and one small person who got to soak up all the love and attention.

But twins happen. And if you got pregnant the way I did, with the best sex money can buy, they happen *a lot.* Living in New York City, capital of putting off motherhood until it's almost too late, it seems I was surrounded by exhausted first-time mothers over thirty-five, barreling into Starbucks with their double-wide Maclarens to grab that 4 P.M. latte that would see them through the kids' bedtime and make them able to carry on a coherent conversation with their husband when he walked through the door. This was not the image of fashionable motherhood I'd created for myself. One baby: a whimsical, portable accessory. Two babies: a smelly, living hell.

At least I'd be amortizing the price of the fertility treatments, I thought, as I vomited for the third time today.

March 14, 2001
Vomiting. Threw up the crackers and ginger ale a friend had recommended.

March 16, 2001

Sent John for ginger and pineapple enzymes from the health food store. Threw up those.

March 18, 2001

Doctor gave me Compazine. Wish I could keep it down. Ditto the metoclopramide and chlorpromazine. I hate taking these drugs. What are they doing to the babies? But then, what is eating nothing doing to the babies?

March 24, 2001

Now taking Zofran, normally given to chemotherapy patients. I no longer hate the drugs. My children can have eyeballs in the middle of their foreheads for all I care, so long as the drugs work. As powerful as Zofran is, it only works moderately. I've lost ten pounds. There was a time when this fact would have made me deliriously happy. That time is not now. Today, my mother said, "You know how desperately I wanted a baby, right? Well, if I'd been this sick with you, I'd have had an abortion."

It's a good time for Sylvia Plath:

METAPHORS
I'm a riddle in nine syllables,
An elephant, a ponderous house,

A melon strolling on two tendrils.
O red fruit, ivory, fine timbers!
This loaf's big with its yeasty rising.
Money's new-minted in this fat purse.
I'm a means, a stage, a cow in calf.
I've eaten a bag of green apples,
Boarded the train there's no getting off.

No getting off.

March 26, 2001

I had to take the ride to my first appointment to the ob-gyn lying flat in the back of a taxi, but still I was exultant. I was a winner! Though probably the cab driver who had to listen to me heaving in the back seat didn't think so. Here, at NYU's high-risk practice, about fifty percent of the patients are having multiple births. There were some young women, too, but the average age here was forty-one. "Hey, compared to some of our patients," said one of the obstetricians, nodding toward a hugely pregnant woman who looked like she could be carrying an AARP card, "you're a spring chicken." I looked around at the many lined faces—tired, but flushed with surprise and happiness. I thought of the technology that got them here. Unnatural? Maybe. But so's the Sistine Chapel, and no one's complaining about that.

March 28, 2001, my birthday.

Ten years ago today, for my thirtieth birthday I went on a camping trip in the Superstition Wilderness, a region of spires and canyons in the Sonora Desert of Arizona. For the first three days it rained. For the next three days it snowed. Rain and snow were not on my agenda for a visit to the desert. We heated rocks in the campfire, then slept by curling around the rocks for warmth. I singed all my clothing. On the day I turned thirty, the cowboys guiding the trip baked me a cake in the ashes and a bunch of strangers sang "Happy Birthday." When we returned to civilization I took a cheap motel room and a cowboy. At least I think he was a cowboy. He could have been a lawyer who owned cows; I'm a little fuzzy on the details. At any rate, he had a Texas drawl and an enormous scar from his collarbone to his sternum. It was the best birthday ever.

Today, my fortieth birthday, I spend lying in bed, staring at a fixed point on the ceiling. Synesthesia, it's called—the confusion of the senses, so that sights have sounds, and sounds have tastes. And in my case, sights have tastes: I'm so nauseated I can't even look at my walls anymore. Normally they are a cheerful cranberry red. Now they are throbbing and taste of rotting meat. Television is out (food commercials), books are impossible (the pages taste like glue). The doctors are talking about hospitalizing me. So I concentrate very hard on my point on the ceiling, and twice a day John brings me oatmeal. I fancy orange juice too, but it hurts too much on its way back up.

April 2, 2001

I want you dead. One of you, if not both of you. I just know you are boys. The weaker sex—at least now. So you will be easier to destroy. As I lie here, wave upon wave of nausea slamming into my throat, I imagine with pleasure lying on the gynecologist's table one last time. He will locate you on the sonogram, your fleck of a heart a shocking *boom, boom, boom,* 160 beats a minute. He will steady his hand. A drop of poison will shiver at the tip of the needle before it's plunged into me. I can't wait. No need to prolong your pain, though. Unlike you, I'm merciful.

Let me watch you squirm like a trout on a hook, then lie silent. I want you both gone forever. You were a terrible idea that everyone said was the *sine qua non,* and like an idiot I believed them. It's taken me $70,000 and countless blood tests, drugs, needles, pokings, and hours filled with dread to bring you here.

Isn't a girl entitled to change her mind?

May 1, 2001

John stands outside the bathroom door as I vomit, shouting helpfully, *"If you don't start eating, you'll have brain-damaged children."* Who knew it would take pregnancy to make me, for the first time in my adult life, thin?

June 12, 2001

"Would you like to know their sex?" the sonogram technician asks me. I already know, in the way I know I have two arms, ten toes, bad eyesight. "Boys, right?" I say.

"No, wait, let me see...no—yes. Both boys."

In a recently published study from the University of Finland, scientists measured the age of death of women from a hundred years ago who'd had sons versus daughters. On average a son shortened a woman's lifespan by thirty-four weeks. Given how I've felt the last few months, I don't care about living that extra thirty-four weeks. So sons are OK by me.

More than OK, actually. I've been ashamed to admit to my girlfriends that I wanted sons. After all, I was a woman who came of age in the seventies, raised on bracing doses of feminism and sexual freedom. At college I never missed a Holly Near concert or a Take Back the Night March; I did my time at women's self-exam nights, where we'd break out the Mateus Rosé, check our cervixes with speculums borrowed from the Women's Health Center, tell ourselves how beautiful we were, and hug. (In truth, the chance I'd perform a gynecological exam on myself in private, much less in company, was zero, but everyone was too drunk to notice I kept my clothes on.) I was going to raise good, strong, proud women, women who would be masters of the system, not dupes of it. Not for my girls the *YM* culture of Britney and Hilary (Duff, not Clinton), Amanda and Beyoncé. They would have no truck with Barbie, Kelly, or the truly terrifying Polly Pocket, with her stretch limo and Sparkle House. (Call me a prude, but I wouldn't want my daughters tending little dollies that dress like ten-dollar whores.) No! I would teach my girls not to be objects, but still to be full, vibrant, sexual beings—to not confuse love with sex, to have relationships only with people they respected, to be as daring and bold in their lives as their mother was timid and fearful.

The pressure was just too much. With boys, all you have to worry about is that one day they might take it into their heads to shoot up the junior high cafeteria.

I do find it disconcerting to think there are things growing inside me that will one day laugh at fart jokes. Still, I sigh with relief when I consider I will probably never have to answer the following question: "*Mom, do these pants make me look fat?*"

When I got home I gave John the news. He nodded and said nothing. John has a son older than I am, whom I've never met. When he was eighteen John and a young, very beautiful Irish girl ended their first date together on a lonely spot high on the moors. There was the wind howling, an old slab of gravestone to lie on. There were tears, second thoughts, and a promise made. John has never backed down from a promise. At nineteen he was married and a father. He did what he could. It was a different time, a time when a young, beautiful woman who was mentally ill only had "a bit of a temper," and if she burned all your books in a bonfire because reading was for the devil or tried to push you down a flight of stairs or came after you with a butcher's knife, well, you were a man, and you didn't talk about such things. If you wanted to leave, you couldn't take your son. You lived in 1950s England. Sons belonged with their mothers.

Being a father had not gone well. Certainly not with a boy. This time John hoped for girls. With girls, at least, he wouldn't feel embarrassed to be tender.

July 1, 2001

Today we were told both boys had "beautiful brains" by two separate sonogram technicians. "Sure, they've got to say something other than, 'Wow, those kids are ug-lee,'" says John, studying the murky, underwater womb footage of

Baby A and Baby B. "Look at that," he whispers, pointing at Baby A. "That one could've crawled out of a swamp."

July 6, 2001

John and I exchange pleasantries but we're lost in our own worlds, each nursing different but equally dread-filled visions of the future. He wanted me to be happy, really he did, but I imagine he's kicking himself for encouraging me to try IVF for the fourth time. He was almost home safe.

But we don't really need to talk to each other about our fears; we don't need to talk at all. Because I have Gary Condit and Chandra Levy for company. This is the summer of the slick, bouffant-haired California congressman and his bit on the side who vanished. Chandra looks eerily like me when I was twenty-four: not beautiful but pleasant and welcoming in that ultra-Semitic style, a look that must have been exotic to the son of a Baptist preacher. My hours between 8 P.M. and midnight are devoted to Larry King, Geraldo Rivera, the Fox News Channel. When I can't sleep now, which is often, I lie back and think, *"Well, it could be worse. I could be Chandra Levy."*

July 13, 2001

My body's doing what it's supposed to do, even if it's doing it sputtering and protesting. In those fleeting moments when I don't feel like a kayak in the middle of a cyclone, I take pleasure in the way I look, that taut belly underneath the fat, like a great set of coil springs on the world's plushest couch. Every time I look in the mirror I hear Charles Laughton saying to Peter Ustinov in *Spartacus*, "You and I have a tendency towards corpulence. Corpulence makes a man reasonable, pleasant, and phlegmatic. Have you noticed that the nastiest of talents are invariably thin?"

So I'd actually be feeling pleased about my body for once, if it weren't for John's tendency to walk up to me, put his hands on my stomach, and shudder. He is not a fan of the pregnant female form. This is unfortunate, since he could be having a much better sex life than he's had in a long time. (God's little joke: when I'm not immobilized with nausea, I am amorous.) I've shown John all the porn Web sites for men who have fetishes for pregnant and lactating women, in the hopes that he would get with the program. So far, no luck. The whole situation spooks him. He seems to think that the moment he springs into action, they'll be glaring at him from the inside.

When I'm calm, I try to jolly him up. "Don't think of them as your children; that sounds like too much of a burden," I say. "Think of them as do-it-yourself grandchildren!" But in moments of anger I think, "*What the fuck?*" The man's getting a gift late in life that only the wealthiest men allow themselves. And not only doesn't he appreciate it; he looks at me as if I've become another person. The woman he married, so obsessed with her work, her books, her social obligations: that is not the gaunt, green-skinned harridan in front of him now.

"I thought we'd have a wonderful life," he says plaintively. "I thought we'd do everything together. I didn't think you'd want children. When everyone else had them, you never looked twice. You never even wanted to hold them."

He was perfectly right, of course. Men look at marriage as a contract: you change, you break the contract. Women look at marriage as a screenplay. You change? Call in rewrite!

"At least you've got what you wanted," he continues. "It's good one of us is happy."

August 7, 2001
My father had a seventy-eighth birthday, and my Uncle Albert a massive stroke. They found him sitting in his easy chair, blinking, stunned, cigarette ash crisping his fingers.

My uncle is a great man and a great musician. Exasperating politically, true; how many times could one maintain a straight face while listening to assertions about what a misunderstood man Newt Gingrich was? Controlling too and wrongheaded about women, as romantics disappointed in love often are; his great totemic villains were Jane Fonda and Gloria Steinem. He was bitter about what he saw as the lack of civility in our culture, which made him reflexively Anglophilic: he loved John, for no better reason than that John is British. He always reeked of old cigarette smoke but would baldly lie to his sisters and insist that he gave up smoking after his first heart attack.

But Uncle Albert was also the kindest of men and, lacking children himself, considered me and my cousins his own. "How's my favorite niece?" he invariably greeted me— and all his other nieces, as I discovered recently. When I was a child he did not think it odd that I wanted to be a herpetologist, and he got me the presents I wanted, presents that were not necessarily suitable for a little girl. One Christmas he came over to the house with a boa constrictor in a burlap sack; for my thirteenth birthday, there was the tarantula. When he heard I was pregnant, I think he was happier than anyone save my mother. At that point, he was already very sick. He told no one, certainly not himself.

Uncle Albert was the person I was depending on to reveal to my children the secret code of men. As a conductor who spent much of his life touring with musicals, he could tear up at the simplicity of Julie Andrews' joy in the first swooping refrain of "I Could Have Danced All Night," or the defiance mixed with the pathos in Paul Robeson's "Old Man River." But he was also the only person in my sports-challenged family who knew what a quarterback sneak was, who could tell the difference between a bunt and a line drive. I hate organized sports passionately, and one of my great fears in having boys was the thought we might suddenly have to become conversant in the season's basket scores of the Knicks' front-line defense. Is "front-line defense" the right sporty term for what those people do, or is that the name of a flea remedy for dogs? I'm not sure, and that's the point. John was certainly no better than I. Although at sixty-seven he still lifted weights four times a week and took pleasure in watching two men on Pay-Per-View beat the crap out of each other, that's where his interest in sports ended. So I always took great comfort in the thought that if my children showed even a glimmer of interest, I could drop them off at Uncle Albert's and drive away, secure in the knowledge that when I returned they would be able to hold their own in one of those manly discussions for which the banter always begins, "Did you watch the game last night?"

Tonight he lay in the hospital bed, one beautiful ropy hand useless, the other gripping my arm ferociously. He searched my eyes and mumbled incoherently. He was sure I could understand him. I couldn't understand a word, but I pretended I did. Not for the first time and certainly not for the last did I hate myself for waiting so long to have children.

49

WHAT FRESH HELL IS THIS? During the twenty-eighth week of my pregnancy, the doctors at NYU noticed something was very wrong.

Dr. Timor, the forbidding, beetle-browed ultrasound specialist from Hungary who resembled Bela Lugosi, pored over my ultrasound. "Ees problem vit your blud," he muttered darkly.

"Ees problem! Bluuuuud!" I drawled to John on the way home. I was so intent on perfecting my Dr. Timor impression that it took a while for me to grasp that there was, in fact, a problem with my blood. A Doppler scan, which measures placental blood flow, showed that one of my placentas was giving out. This is what placentas do; they are organs with a planned obsolescence. However, they're supposed to hold up for forty weeks, maybe thirty-eight for twins. But because one of mine was packing it up early, the blood flow to Baby A had slowed from a river to a trickle, meaning that oxygen and nutrients might be in short supply. If the babies were not delivered right away, one would likely be stillborn. On the other hand, if both were delivered right away, I would have two children who, they estimated, weighed 2.5 pounds apiece. Their lungs would probably be too immature to function on their own. That would mean weeks and perhaps months in the neonatal ICU unit on respirators, and with respirators came the possibility that air would be blown too forcefully into tiny lungs, resulting in ruptured blood vessels and possible brain damage.

No one could understand my hesitation. "We could deliver them today, right now," my obstetrician told me. Dr. Saltzman was a thoughtful, conscientious man given to nervous jokes about his height and girth. He was a Republican, but still I found it in my heart to love him. "I know two and a half pounds sounds small to you, but to the neonatal doctors those are big boys."

What if I waited? Well, one could die. And there was a strong possibility the other placenta would stop working too. I could be playing double or nothing: *both* could be still-born. But. If they were born now, there was a good chance of a lifetime of problems, or at the very least some mild, subtle brain damage. Why have two damaged children when there's a good chance of one perfect one?

If I'd known them as I know them now, I would have made a different choice. I'd have been in love. I'd have wanted them both. I would have had them delivered at twenty-eight weeks. And they'd probably be dead, because they were far smaller than the doctors knew.

But I didn't know that at the time. All I knew was, Let's roll the dice.

And so began the weeks of scans, the smear of chilly electro-conducting gel on the belly, the daily wait for good news or disaster. Every other day for the next six weeks, John and I sat in the ultrasound waiting room, checking to see if Twin A and Twin B were still moving. One day neither of them would budge. I poked them, coughed, drank cold water…nothing worked. The tech was on the verge of calling her supervisor when John stuck his face next to my stomach and, in his basso profundo, bellowed, *"Move, you bloody little bastards."* And they did. Possibly because I almost fell off the table.

Until this point I had thought of them as Scottish soccer hooligans: there was hardly a moment in the day I wasn't being kicked by one or both. But now I waited, not to feel the kicks, but to feel their cessation—the sudden absence of internal agitation that would signal not only a death but what I felt was my own selfishness. Who was I to say that one healthy life was more valuable than two compromised ones? As the weeks went by, I noticed that Dr. Saltzman's nails, normally short, were bitten to the quick. "You make me nervous," he said.

A few weeks went by, and the other placenta began to fail too. I told myself maybe it was time to get this over with, and I asked if I could have a cesarean on September 12, 2001. It was an auspicious day, I thought, the birthday of one of my favorite writers, H. L. Mencken.

On September 11, right before 9:00 A.M., I woke up to what sounded like a plane flying into my window. I barely had time to think, "Hm, that's not something you hear over Bleecker Street," before there was a thud and people on the street screaming. My bedroom window looks west and south to the World Trade Center. There was a plume of smoke. I turned on the news.

Was I thinking, "My God, the world's just changed irrevocably"? No. My only thought was, *"Damn. Tomorrow's not going to be a good day to have a baby."*

And so I waited.

September 14, 2001

Dreamt last night that we were under martial law, and one of the first rules instituted was that dogs could not go outside without wearing lipstick. I was frantically applying the lipstick to my golden retriever, Monty, and he was licking it off, and I was sure he'd be killed.

Nothing feels right.

September 16, 2001

It's interesting how every writer in town has, within the course of five days, managed to turn around a clever fifteen hundred words on the unique depth of their sorrow. It's natural for publications to want stories and for people to jostle to write them. I just don't think you can have it both ways: claim you're utterly devastated, and then whirl around and snap to for the pitch. That's rather like the vulture sending a Hallmark sympathy card to the roadkill's family just before lunch.

I have already gotten two calls from two different magazines, asking if I know any attractive, photogenic women between the ages of twenty and thirty-five who've been traumatized by the WTC accident. Someone should start an agency of tragedy-stricken supermodels. Those girls would clean up.

ON SEPTEMBER 19 I was admitted to the hospital with a possible diagnosis of preeclampsia, an abnormal rise in blood pressure related to pregnancy that could further compromise the placenta or could cause everything from swelling to (in extreme cases) stroke. I knew I didn't have preeclampsia. I knew I was just pissed. I'd just had a horrendous fight with a friend. Several years earlier she had suffered a postpartum depression severe enough to land her in a mental hospital. Now she was convinced I would suffer the same fate. "Don't wait; start your Prozac now," Andrea urged.

I explained that while I was happy the electroshock therapy and lithium had done the job for her, I was less than enthusiastic about taking a mind-altering drug for a condition I didn't yet have. But Andrea was not one to be easily thwarted. She got the number of a close friend of mine—a woman I also worked for, whom Andrea never met—and tried to convince her that my mental health was precarious. I wasn't prepared for motherhood, Andrea said; I didn't know what I was getting into, and I needed a good talking-to. Would Nancy explain to me that antidepressants could be my salvation? Andrea swore Nancy to secrecy—which pretty much guaranteed that Nancy, chortling, would be on the phone to me ten minutes later.

While I didn't think I was a candidate for postpartum depression, I was now an excellent candidate for prepartum homicidal rage. By the time I got to the doctor's office, my blood pressure was 170/110. The next thing I knew I was in a hospital room, saving all my pee in a jug. The bathroom had to be shared with four other women, who were also part of the pee conservation program. Our jugs were lined up like tubby soldiers.

The second night I awoke to find the toilet brimming with blood. It was a scene out of *The Shining*. At this point I was beyond being repulsed. I just told the nurse, who wondered aloud whose blood it was. "Oh wait, that must be Mary," she said. "She's postpartum. She's *allowed* to bleed."

I stayed in the hospital for a week. My friend Steven came and played Scrabble with me and let me win. John brought me food I couldn't eat. My mother called every ten minutes. I fumed.

On September 25 an ultrasound revealed that the babies had stopped growing altogether. I had approximately fifteen minutes' warning before Dr. Saltzman had his hands buried in my uterus, cracking bad jokes: "Hey, Judith, now I can say I know you inside *and* out!" John stayed away, as we had agreed, though during the operation I had a little pang of regret that as my children came into the world it was a stranger whose eyes I gazed into.

I spent the entire operation waiting to hear two phrases Steven, a physician, told me were code words obstetricians used during delivery: FLK and FLM. FLK = "funny-looking-kid," code for something looking wrong. FLM is often the reassuring reply to FLK. It means "Well, yes, but don't worry—funny-looking-mother."

The nurses had removed my glasses, so I didn't see them clearly before they were whisked away to the neonatal intensive care unit. John and I had already come up with suitably British names. Since baby naming was the one subject we could discuss during my pregnancy that did not leave me in tears, we'd spent untold hours on the subject. Fortunately he had curbed my undoubtedly hormone-addled desire to name them after Brontë characters. Few infants can carry off Heathcliff and Rochester. On the other hand, I got to partially squelch John's fondness for Roman emperors, which meant that my children would not have to go through life as

Tarquinius and Octavius. But at any rate, I wish I'd seen them long enough to decide which would get which name.

My entire family—mother, father, cousins, aunt, uncle—suddenly materialized, but all I remember is shivering violently under a blanket while John held my hand and looked grim. Was it me? The babies? The hospital? All three, I suppose. John had spent so many years sitting in hospital rooms.

WHEN JOHN WAS IN HIS EARLY TWENTIES he worked as an engineer for the coal mining industry and became their youngest union trade organizer. But as his singing career took off, he could no longer stay in Great Britain. He needed to move to Italy. He asked Kathleen to move with him. She refused. She also refused to grant him a divorce. Sometimes she let his son see him, sometimes she did not. He moved to Italy.

There he met Amy. She was also an opera singer, seventeen years his senior. Amy was as sweet-natured and sunny as Kathleen was glowering and dangerous. She was also a classical beauty of her era, looking rather like a blond Rita Hayworth. One day, after they were together for about a year, Amy turned to John and asked, "Do you think I'm pretty? You've never really said anything." He made the fatal mistake of hesitating. Her eyes filled with tears.

What had stopped him was not that for one second he questioned her desirability—to him, that was self-evident—

but that for so long he had seen her as just Amy, the girl with the voice and the mind he loved. He had ceased to consider the menthol-blue eyes, the patrician slope of her jaw, the way her fine nostrils flared when she was enthused about something. Of course she was beautiful, he told her. But to him, she was just . . . Amy.

And she continued to be just Amy, when the cancer ravaged her perfect body, when her hair fell out and her face bloated and her bones snapped if she moved too quickly. At the time she was diagnosed with metastatic breast cancer she was given about four months to live. Under John's care, she proceeded to live another eighteen years. She died in 1989, not of the cancer but of a massive stroke. The day she was cremated was one of those crisp, icy December mornings when the sun is brilliant and it hurts to draw a breath. As John left the funeral home with Amy's ashes in a box under his arm, a trail of fine, dry snowflakes fell on the box. He looked up; there wasn't a cloud in the sky. Almost immediately the snow stopped.

Flash forward four years: John and I were eloping, on a similarly brilliant, cloudless November day. Just as the ceremony ended snow began to fall—huge, powdery flakes from nowhere. Just as suddenly, the snow vanished.

John is not a religious man. Still, from these two incidents he deduced that wherever Amy was, she was offering her benediction.

AS I LAY IN BED, DOZING AND SHIVERING, I thought it would have been nice if John had made with the flowers, maybe cracked a smile. He didn't have to *be* happy, but couldn't he fake it for my sake?

But then I thought of Amy, and John, and eighteen years of sitting in hospitals all over the country—all over the world. Amy had wanted children. She couldn't have them. Maybe John was thinking of Amy too.

September 25, 2001

Is it a bad omen already that I planned for my children to be born on H. L. Mencken's birthday and instead they're born on the birthday of Michael Douglas and Catherine Zeta-Jones? No matter. Despite the doctors' dire predictions, I'm told these two new people, Henry Edmund and Augustus John Snowdon, are actually OK, though at three pounds two ounces and three pounds eleven ounces respectively, they barely add up to one regulation-size baby. They were far smaller than the doctors had thought. If I'd gone ahead and had them delivered at twenty-eight weeks instead of thirty-four, they would probably have each weighed less than a pound and a half. They would probably not have made it. Good thing I didn't love them then. Love would've killed them.

I can't see them yet. They're in the neonatal ICU and I've got too much to do here in postpartum, what with my new career of pressing the morphine-delivery button every 30 seconds. But here's something good: for the first day in seven months, I didn't throw up.

September 26, 2001, morning
What do you mean I'm supposed to get up and move around? Fuck off.

September 26, 2001, noon
For some reason my blood platelet levels were down, a condition I passed on to Henry and Augustus. So this morning I was told both babies received platelet transfusions in the middle of the night to prevent internal bleeding. Henry's count is now up to 300,000, which is fine; Gus's is in the mid-90,000s and climbing. The doctors will do a full body scan next week, but they say the possibility of internal bleeding is remote since platelets were given right away.

Maybe it was the morphine, but I was perfectly confident all would be well. At least I was until a social worker knocked on my door. "I want you to know this is a safe place to discuss all the anxieties you must have," she said, holding my hand and stroking it. Hello, I did not have terrible anxiety *until you mentioned I should about thirty seconds ago.*

LET GO OF MY HAND, YOU JACKAL. I flash back to
Woody Allen's nightmare in *Annie Hall,* where he is being
chased by a monster with the body of a giant crab and the
head of a social worker.

Here's the thing I can't wrap my mind around. How is it
possible someone—two people, in fact—will call me
"Mother"? It seems like such a huge mix-up, because a) I am
really fifteen years old; the forty-year-old haggard woman
you see before you is just an unsightly mirage; and b) I
shouldn't be trusted with a favorite pair of shoes, let alone a
human life.

September 26, 2001, 5:00
Despite their tiny size, both are breathing on their own.
Henry, the tinier one, has that patented take-me-to-your-
leader look of preemies but is sucking milk like a regular
baby. Gus is still being fed through a tube. To counteract
their jaundice both are on light therapy. They are wearing
tiny hospital-issued caps that say, "I got my first hug at
NYU." But the writing on the caps is flowing and flowery; I
read it as "I got my first flug at NYU" and had to ask the
nurse why they had needed a flug. I though it was some sort
of medical procedure.

Not only do these small people not look related to me or
John, they don't look related to each other. Henry is bald

and pale as a grub, with skin that immediately flushes crimson with the slightest exertion. His head is the size of a cantaloupe, and he's ravenous. His nose is large and bulbous, thus dashing my hopes that my nose job could have somehow become embedded in my DNA. Augustus, who's so mellow he has to be jostled while eating to keep him from lapsing into a coma, has a thicket of black hair that stands up like a bottlebrush and an olive complexion like no one in either of our families. John will not shut up about how he looks suspiciously like Dr. Grifo.

"You'll be taking them home as soon as they reach four pounds," the NICU nurse tells me cheerfully. Four pounds? The roast chicken I had last week for dinner was bigger than that. And I'm supposed to do what? *Bathe* them? I am pretty sure if I place them on a moist towelette they'll drown.

Growing up in Scarsdale during the seventies—what I now think of as the *Ice Storm* years—my baby-sitting experience consisted of arriving after the kids went to sleep and rummaging through their parents' porn collection. Baby-sitting is how I first read *The Story of O* and learned that not only cops but accountants and periodontists may own handcuffs. I lied about my age when I baby-sat. The boy I sat for most often was, unbeknownst to his parents, six months older than I was. I told them I was sixteen; I was, in fact, twelve. Gary had just turned thirteen. He always kept me sitting on his bed, talking way past his bedtime. He sat close. I think he was on to me.

Children scared me, even as a child. What were they going to do next? There were lots of bodily fluids that might fly in your direction at any time. Babies made you into a befuddled contestant in the game show from hell: spin the wheel and you land...on...sweet smile?...no... mellifluous chortle?...no...*vomit. Bleah.* And then there was the way mothers would hand me their infants, who would invariably take one look at me and burst into tears. *"They're like dogs in horror movies,"* I thought. *"They can sense fear."*

I hover over Henry and Augustus's incubators, watching them glow under the sinister ultraviolet lights. The nurses tell me I can hold them, but I'm afraid. I touch the palms of their hands, and they do The Grasp. Nature or God, take your pick, declared that all newborns grab your finger. It is only a reflex, neither a sign of affection nor even an acknowledgment of our existence. I believe it's a reflex whose express purpose is to endear them to us. What if they had a reflex to flick away our hands dismissively or, instead of staring at us intently, to roll their eyes like teenagers? There'd be far fewer babies.

Their skin is almost translucent. If I pick them up, it might peel off in my hands like a layer of boiled onion.

CHANGED DIAPERS THIS AFTERNOON. I was ready with several boxes of surgical gloves for this eventuality. Having barely held a baby before having my own, let alone changed one, I was sure I'd be too squeamish to do this bare-handed. I was wrong. They're much less gross than all other babies. Odd.

After the diaper change, it took me approximately twenty minutes to put a onesie on Henry. I told the nurse not to help me. At first, I somehow fit it on him like it was a straitjacket. I untangled him, but I managed to twist part of the outfit into his mouth, like a gag. The nurse leaned over and said to me gently, "What do you do for a living?" I said, "Well, here's a hint: *it doesn't involve fine motor skills.*"

It's not a question of whether I will kill them; it's just a question of how. Drowning? Tumbling off the changing table? Will the dog think they're food?

FRIENDS AND FAMILY VISIT, and I'm caught between the curious pleasure of showing off what came out of me and embarrassment at having turned out tiny creatures so pink and raw and unformed. They remind me of nothing so much as baby gerbils. It seems such a poor effort on my part. If only I could put them back in and let them bake a while longer.

Elizabeth breezes in. She is a woman of many gifts, not the least of which is her inability to see the obvious, if the obvious is in any way bad. She is the most optimistic person I know, utterly genuine even when she's wrong. Being friends with Elizabeth is like hanging out with your own personal sun.

"Where are they?" she demands hungrily. Elizabeth is the eldest in a family of six. Under those conditions you either love babies or you hate them. She loves them. Hesitatingly, I show them to her; she coos over Augustus and then immediately hones in on Henry. With his enormous cranium and sparrowlike body, Henry had passed homely and gone directly to frightening. "That," says Elizabeth decisively, "is a beautiful baby. Look at that noble brow! He radiates intelligence." For years Elizabeth ran a parenting magazine; she has spent much of her life around small children. I run my fingers over Henry's bald scalp, shuddering only slightly as I touch the soft spot that yields like the bruise on a peach. Beautiful? Well, who am I to argue?

I'm afraid I rushed Elizabeth out of the hospital quickly. I didn't want her to see me cry.

September 27, 2001

Home again. I left a day early with a cheerful wave and a prescription for Percodan. Pain, schmain. I am Master of the Universe!

Last night I had my recurring dream where I forget to feed everyone in the house. In the dream I realize what I'm doing, but I can't help myself. My boa constrictor stares at me grimly, willing me to put my arm into his cage so he can attack; he's lost all hope of a meal. (Actually, I don't have my boa, Julius Squeezer, anymore. And I don't want to think too carefully about what the appearance of a ravenous snake says about the last nine months of my sex life with John.) The plants wither; Monty, my golden retriever, lies in a corner breathing hard, his bones visible under his dull, matted coat.

Monty wakes me up in his usual manner, wagging and shoving a filthy sneaker in my face. His red coat is glossy, his nose cold and wet. I am rigid with anxiety. When will Henry and Augustus be home?

THE NICU AT MIDNIGHT is as serene as an aquarium; life bubbles quietly to the surface. Who are these three-pound humans we're supposed to take care of for the next twenty years? I don't know. But I do have some hopes for them already.

> In a few years you will get exactly the bike you want, and it will fill you with joy for a long time.

One day, you will sit down to build something. It will be a complex project. You will take your time, do it right, and when you are done, it will work just like they said it would.

You will confront a bully and he will fold on the spot.

You will eat an Ess-a-Bagel. And pastrami at Katz's and a porterhouse at Peter Luger's. You'll drink coffee out of a tin cup made on a campfire on a beach in Santorini, and it'll be the best coffee you've ever had, even though in reality it's harsh muddy crap.

You will read *Lolita* and never be the same.

Ditto to hearing Beethoven's "Appassionata" and seeing *Sunset Boulevard.*

You will walk out of the house and get in the car and drive away by yourself.

You will sleep naked between crisp, freshly laundered sheets.

Someone will kiss you, and it will matter.

One day, your parents will look you in the eye and tell you how proud they are of you. They will mean every word and it will fill your heart to bursting.

Plath again. Always Plath, when I think about children. "I'm no more your mother/Than the cloud that distills a mirror to reflect its own slow/ Effacement at the wind's hand."

I ask John what he wishes for his children. "I wish you'd eaten normally and they were bigger," he says, Gus's spider monkey paw clasping John's bulbous thumb.

September 29, 2001

Far worse than the cesarean incision, not quite as bad as eight months of nausea is the pain of engorged breasts when milk comes in. Today I lay in bed, shaking; it was all I could do to put a sports bra and ice pack on them and crawl back into bed. I remind myself I will never have to feel like this again.

When I confessed to Andrea that I had no intention of breastfeeding, it was as if I'd said, "I have no intention of feeding them. At all." Even before I knew I was having twins (and therefore could pretty much demand a cesarean), I knew I wanted the Zsa Zsa Gabor birth experience—a C-section with as many drugs as possible. If I could have talked them into knocking me out entirely instead of giving me the epidural, I would have done it gladly. I never understood friends who said they wanted to be alert and present for the birth experience. Why? If I said, "Hey, you're having your appendix removed; don't you want to feel what that's like?" I suspect the majority would say no. So what's so life-affirming about this particular brand of searing pain?

With breastfeeding, it was the same thing. Generations of children have grown up without breast milk, yet if today a woman suggests she doesn't want to breastfeed because it's uncomfortable (at first) and inconvenient (*"Honey, I want to leave the house for four hours. Break out the robo-milker"*) there's something unnatural about her. Maybe it's that I'm not so great with transitions—the notion that one day your breasts are sex objects, and the next day they're a buffet. Or maybe it's that I resent breastfeeding's fashionableness, typified by an interview I read a few years ago with the singer/actress Brandy, who was pregnant with her first child. "I'm going to be a real mommy," she said. "I'm going to nurse." So what are nonnursing women? Mommies *manquées*?

I understand that breast milk is ideal, that it has antibodies that strengthen a baby's immune system. But for that I have the dog. I figure that having a golden retriever lick your head every day must have immune system–enhancing qualities. For the women who find breastfeeding intimate and pleasurable, great. I wish I felt that way. I don't. I feel, *"I am not food."*

September 30, 2001
John and I want to do parental things for Henry and Gus, but we're still at sea. We can't hold them for very long; their premature nervous systems are still jangly. Besides, they are lying in a tangle of wires, and I keep giving myself a

coronary watching Gus flatline when I mistakenly detach his heart monitor. I weep my way through several readings of *The Runaway Bunny* ("You will always be my bunny..." *sob*), and John recites from memory the first chapter of Dickens' *A Christmas Carol: "Marley was dead, to begin with..."* With his booming operatic voice we soon have quite a little crowd gathered. Gus seems to enjoy it. He sighs under the bilirubin lights.

October 1, 2001

It's never too early to become a Momzilla.

Momzillas are mothers whose lives are defined by their children, and more specifically, by their children's accomplishments. My friend Andrea is a momzilla. Gypsy Rose Lee's mother was the ur-momzilla. And today I noticed several momzillas roaming the NICU unit, looking for fresh meat.

"What were your boys' Apgar scores?" the woman with the son in the isolette next to mine asks. Brad Johns had just shocked her hair into white-blondness; her Juicy Couture sweats were still slightly damp from Pilates class. "Carter's was a ten." At this point I don't even know what an Apgar score is, but I've decided it's something like the SATs. Gus and Henry got a seven and an eight.

"Eleven," I say.

October 2, 2001

One of the many unforeseen advantages of having as one's
friends the editors of the country's big beauty and fashion
magazines is that I now have enough outrageously expensive
baby clothing and bath products to open my own swish
little Madison Avenue shop. Nancy threw the shower, and
Elizabeth held it at her apartment. The shower had been
postponed three times, what with the various pregnancy
difficulties. But now, with Henry and Gus in the hospital
instead of in me, I was thrilled that for the first time in
eight months I could enjoy food. And what food: lobster
risotto cakes, smoked duck on toasted brioche, rosemary
bruschetta with Jerusalem artichoke puree, pizza with
robiola, arugula, and truffle oil—not to mention the
miniature hamburgers. The caterer is my friend Catherine,
who was reduced to catering my party after leaving her job
as Donatella Versace's personal chef. "Donatella, she's
Italian, they have beautiful manners, but the Americans she
surrounds herself with . . . you can't imagine," Catherine
sighs. There was a little contretemps with one of the
hangers-on, who had woken her up and demanded an egg-
white omelette at three in the morning. From there things
got ugly. "These people, they'll put anything up their
nose, but God forbid they have a little cholesterol,"
Catherine added.

Donatella's loss is my gain, I thought, as I thanked God for such kind friends and sucked back another peach bellini.

October 3, 2001

Today it occurs to me that soon I'll have to find somewhere to put Henry and Gus. I do not live on the prairie in a Willa Cather novel. A drawer won't do.

It's not like we were completely unprepared to welcome two children home. After all, we did go looking for a house in Westchester when I found out I was pregnant with twins. And when several weekends of house hunting left me shaky and weeping, overwhelmed with dread at the prospect of moving back to the suburbs where I grew up—and having to live in the same house with my husband, no less—I overpaid lavishly for the apartment right above mine. I will break through, putting in a staircase and finally creating the glorious New York City apartment of my dreams! Someday! If I ever make enough money for the construction!

But meanwhile, I have this problem.

I'VE BEEN LIVING IN A STATE OF DENIAL serious enough to ensure that I have not one practical baby supply in this house. I don't know what I was thinking. That I'd go shopping on my way to the hospital? Or that all I needed was a two-year supply of Petit Bateau?

In the last forty-eight hours John has managed to assemble two cribs and place them in the living room. My cousin Amy went out and fetched three hundred dollars' worth of diapers, wipes, clothes, bottles, moisturizers, and burp cloths, plus a first aid kit in such complicated packaging that I imagined a baby expiring while I attempted to rip open the bottle of ipecac with my teeth. I placed the two baby swings, with their six variable speed settings, side by side in the living room now turned nursery. (In the future I'd come to think of them as the Neglect-O-Matics.)

I went back to the hospital to visit the babies. Just when I thought I'd conceived of every current and future terror, a nurse turned to me and said, "Mrs. Snowdon, be careful about getting your long hair near the kids. If any of those hairs get into their diapers, they could twist around their testicles and cut off the blood supply."

October 4, 2001

Henry has managed to eat his way out of the hospital, making it to a whopping four pounds in one week. So, terrifyingly, he is home. Luckily, however, Yvonne has come to live on our couch. Yvonne specializes in twins and triplets. She is large and quiet and still. When she moves, it is usually to turn up the volume on CNN, to which she is addicted. It is the only television she watches, and she watches twenty-four hours a day. She is not happy with the current state of global politics. There is a lot of muttering about needing to "smite" the evil terrorists, and when Henry is asleep she comes into my bedroom/office to report on what's happening in Kandahar. I think of her as the Bad News Baby Nurse.

But when her eyes aren't glued to CNN, she is effortlessly feeding and calming a crying child. She is so calm and competent that in less than forty-eight hours I am afraid to disrupt her by, say, playing with my baby. This morning she informed me that Henry shouldn't be picked up too much at the beginning, other than for feeding and a little cuddling, because otherwise he won't be able to settle down by himself. So I lie in wait to hold him. Yvonne takes a shower...quick! Grab the baby! If she goes to the laundry room...sneak over to crib, cuddle! When she went to the grocery store for a few minutes, she returned to find me picking up Henry for no reason whatsoever while he was still asleep. I froze like a dog caught sinking his teeth into the Thanksgiving turkey.

She seems completely besotted by infants. But humans over three months? She's not so sure. She is fond of John; being male and British, he can be excused any incompetence. But she seems to take a pretty dim view of me. Yvonne grew up on a farm in rural Jamaica with eight brothers and sisters. There was no running water; she and two sisters shared a bed. Every morning by 4:30 A.M., she was out in the fields, tending the goats. I grew up in Scarsdale, where for their sixteenth birthdays most of my friends were given a choice between getting a new car or a rhinoplasty. There was a notable paucity of goats.

Well, at least I've done one thing that meets with her approval: I haven't circumcised my children. Cautiously, she asks me why I haven't done it. She knows I'm Jewish. I explain that neither I nor my parents were religious, and John feels circumcision is a form of mutilation. Therefore, since it wasn't important to me, I respected his wishes on this matter.

This was a mistake. Yvonne is a deeply religious Baptist. Here, she reasons, is a Jewish girl who nevertheless didn't circumcise her sons: *carpe diem!* I now have several pamphlets next to my bed with titles like "The Grace That Saves." Yvonne is taking a correspondence course to become a minister. I think I'm her practice soul.

October 7, 2001

I have taken this glorious nausea-free afternoon to do something I haven't done in nine months: dye my hair. God knows if hair coloring really makes any difference to a developing fetus. But we older mothers, good Do-Bees all, want to do the responsible thing, and not dyeing our hair is an easier sacrifice than doing without the daily coffee or glass of wine or other fashionably verboten pleasures. (Wine only hurts developing babies if you live in the United States. In France it makes them smarter and, apparently, capable of tying neck scarves.)

One of the many surprises of pregnancy at forty was the discovery that I'm as gray as my ninety-five-year-old neighbor. If I didn't look haggard enough from the horrors of my pregnancy, the two-inch roots gave away the game. Being gray and pregnant was bad enough, but I also had that distinctly crazy-old-downtown-lady-taking-poetry-classes-at-the-New-School-because-she-wants-to-find-herself frizz.

But no more. I am my original unoriginal reddish brown. I don't look much younger. But at least I don't look like cats are my only friends.

October 16, 2001

Augustus still weighs a shade under four pounds, but his spitting up is under control and they decided he was eating enough to come home. Yesterday, bringing him back from the hospital all bundled up in his car seat, I noticed he looked like Chucky, minus the bloody facial scars. People were stopping and saying, "Look how tiny he is—like a little doll!" But I believe they were thinking, "Oh my God! *Run away, run away!*"

When I brought Gus into the house, I was startled by how large Monty looked. His head is larger than Gus's whole body. Suddenly he resembled a polar bear with a golden sheen more than a retriever. Fortunately, Monty has greeted the tiny usurpers by ignoring them—unless they are covered in formula, at which point he materializes from nowhere to lick them off. This makes Yvonne panicky. She does not make fine distinctions between, say, *golden retriever* and *timber wolf.*

I can't sense much about Gus yet, other than the fact that for someone who still doesn't top the scales at four pounds, he's really quite a handsome fellow, russet-skinned and dark-eyed and smiley. Well, perhaps it's not a smile; perhaps his lips just naturally incline upwards, like a porpoise. He seems to like show tunes; I played all of *Kiss Me Kate* for him this afternoon. But with Henry—pale, weird-looking, otherworldly—there is the disturbing sense of someone trapped and struggling in that scrawny body. As I am reading him *The Tale of Mr. Jeremy Fisher*, he wakes up, stares at me, then at the book, then at me again. When I finish reading he closes his eyes. He rests his hands on his forehead while he sleeps, looking like Rodin's *The Thinker*—and like his father, who sleeps in exactly the same posture.

John tells me not to discuss my theories of personality with anyone, for fear they'll think I'm losing my mind. "They eat, they sleep, they defecate, period," he says. I wish he'd stop referring to Henry as "Brain Stem."

October 18, 2001

Are optimism and pessimism hardwired? I can't help thinking they are, given how Augustus (the optimist) and Henry (the pessimist) greet the world already:

> *Gus:* Listen, the formula's great. Feed me whenever you get around to it, I'm in no rush. No, no, take your time, really. There's always plenty more where that came from. Diaper change? Whenever. I'm not going anywhere!
>
> *Henry:* This is *the last time you'll feed me, ever. Right? Right?* No, it's OK, you can tell me the truth, this is the last bottle I'll ever get, so I need it *right now.* No, wait, don't go away, why have all the lights gone out? Oh, it's because *I'm blind!* I'm not blind? It was just my hat over my eyes? Oh man, that was a close one. Now, can you change my diaper, please? Please? I *hate dirt.* I am *never going to eat and I'm probably going blind and I'll be sitting in this dirty diaper until I die.* Wait, there's more

food? And I'm being changed? Whew. OK. OK. But then *this* is the last bottle you'll ever give me, right?

As some sort of evolutionarily adaptive insurance that I will not throttle him, Henry has perfected that look of baby gratitude, enormous wide eyes boring into me, guzzling the bottle with grunts of pleasure, as if to say, *"Thank you thank you thank you, if you'd waited one more minute before feeding me my head was going to explode."*

His fist is a soft plum in my mouth.

October 31, 2001

"What are you doing?" asks John.

What did it look like I was doing? I was just your average forty-year-old woman in a Spiderman suit, taking her two pumpkins out for a stroll. I love that Henry and Gus were supposed to be born today, and though they made their entrance on life's stage a bit early and couldn't yet go outdoors to appreciate the Greenwich Village pandemonium, I saw no reason they couldn't begin their trick-or-treating career now.

This has always been my favorite holiday. If I lied upward about my age in order to baby-sit, I lied downward to trick-or-treat. I rationalized being the only sixteen-year-old knocking on doors in Scarsdale by telling myself I was getting that much more use out of the expensive jodhpurs, jacket, and riding boots my parents bought me. In college I reluctantly substituted going door-to-door for actual parties, where I compensated for my lack of costume-designing talent with outfits that were brilliant, even if they required explanation. One year I ransacked all the laundry rooms, removing the fluff from the dryers; I glued it to my body, then went around to people at the school party and held onto their arms. When they looked at me in understandable alarm, I explained that I was lint clinging to their sweaters.

Fuck you. It was a great costume.

At the point where I had run out of excuses to run around in the dark asking strangers for candy, I began to be sad about not having children. For the last seven years I had spent Halloween night trying to have a good time, buying bags and bags and bags of candy and accosting children on the street to give it away; their parents always held their hands a little tighter when they saw me coming. By nine I'd always be in bed, defeated.

But by God, not tonight! Just because they were five weeks old, I was not to be denied! I wrestled them into their pumpkin suits—the first purchase I had made after I found out I was pregnant—and pushed them around my apartment building. Total haul: eight Kit-Kat bars, four 3 Musketeers, three boxes of Goobers, two Charleston Chews, four

Butterfingers, and nine bags of M&Ms, six plain and three with peanuts.

There was some killjoy giving out boxes of raisins. Henry and Gus hate those kinds of people.

November 3, 2001

"You're not going to the polls today, are you?" Every November on Election Eve since I turned eighteen my mother has called, only half-jokingly, to urge me not to vote: "I hate that you're canceling me out."

The thing that's a little disconcerting about my mother is that in her behavior to individuals she is the kindest and gentlest woman, and in her political beliefs she is a right wing frootbat. A contributor to Judicial Watch and avid reader of *The Weekly Standard* (a magazine to which she keeps sending me subscriptions, which may explain why I still get "personalized" greetings and requests for large sums of cash from Dick Cheney), my mother for years could not have a conversation with me that did not revisit her theory of how the Clintons killed Vince Foster. While my father is deeply conservative and we disagree on virtually everything, I could always argue with him on some plane that made sense. With my mother... well, it's difficult to discuss the fairness of the criminal justice system with a person whose first comment, upon hearing of someone who's been accused

81

of a crime, is inevitably, "He should be let loose naked in Central Park with a pack of pit bulls." Mom has a sweet little voice, which always sounds odd propounding her latest solution to the Mideast crisis: "We have to nuke the whole region," she says—adding, curiously, "That's what it will take to save Israel." I've never been able to convince her that getting extramarital blow jobs is not on the same scale of wrongdoing as, say, decimating a country that has not attacked you because you need to control its oil. "At least George W. didn't cheat on his wife," she replies.

Today she took special pleasure in urging me not to vote because she got to add the thought I know she's been harboring for a long time: "I think Henry and Gus will be Republicans."

November 8, 2001

I've been so smug about my mastery of this baby business. Everyone has been telling me how well rested I look—not like a new mother at all! And it's been true. John's been in England for a few weeks, but I felt, "Who needs him?" The kids are spotless, and so is their room; even in this tiny apartment, I've found a place for everything. I felt fit, healthy; I had time to get a manicure and a brow wax. I was a whole woman.

Then Yvonne took a night off.

The babies took this opportunity to have a growth spurt, which made them unsatisfied with twice the usual amount of formula we normally feed them. Yvonne's feeding-every-three-hours schedule was shot. Somehow last night I was feeding one or the other for five hours straight. I don't know what happened. By the time I had one fed and burped, the other wanted just a little more . . . so I fed a little more, and then the other was hungry—wash, rinse, repeat. At some point I must have lost track of who was eating what, and I apparently overdid it with Gus, who reminded me of my error by projectile vomiting over his new footsie pajamas. Then he was hungry again, and suddenly it seemed not unreasonable to trade them to the man on the corner for an ounce of weed and a Colt 45.

Yvonne is on her way back here now. I can't let her see the house like this. Burp rags and bottles and pacifiers everywhere: it looks like an army of babies exploded in my apartment. I am so unhinged that as I'm writing this, I've just fished out of a bowl of cereal I'm eating what may or may not be a large black insect. I'm eating the cereal anyway. It's the first thing I've had to eat all day, and it's easier to eat it than to hunt around the kitchen for something else.

Did I mention that while I was bathing Henry, he slipped out of my grasp like a greased pig?

Yvonne was supposed to be here for two weeks, at $250 a day. A ridiculous expense, I thought, but after all, I needed to learn this job of mothering. After two weeks... well, that seemed such a short time. I needed to learn *more.* Now she's been here for a month. I don't care if I have to liquidate an IRA to keep her here. I'm not going through another night like that again.

November 12, 2001

If I hear John use the words "woman's work" one more time to describe caring for Henry and Gus, I may have to mail him some anthrax. He will not diaper. He will not bathe. "I come from a different generation," he intones. "*Yes,*" I think to myself in my less charitable moments, "*and thank goodness your generation is dying out.*"

On the other hand, without him I wouldn't be able to operate any of the accessories necessary for child rearing. Thus far, I've managed to be completely stymied by car seats, folding strollers, and Baby Bjorns. I have hundreds of thousands of dollars' worth of education from Ivy League schools, but I am sadly lacking in the engineering degree necessary to operate the Diaper Genie. There's something disturbing about how all those diapers fit in that squat plastic canister; it's like watching twenty circus clowns climb into a Volkswagen. I've resigned myself to never being able to insert or remove the canister of plastic wrap. But at least I've mastered the actual process of Genie diaper ingestion: you put in the diaper, twist, and repeat endlessly, and at the end of the day you wrestle a long lumpy poo-snake into yet another container of environment-destroying plastic.

Diaper Genies: the work of Satan.

Meanwhile, I can't seem to buy the diapering technology my friend Jessica suggested and I've decided I must have: a couple of soft ankle cuffs attached by a rope to a pulley overhead, which is then attached to a foot pedal. Place the baby's ankles in the cuffs, step on the pedal, and the legs lift up, leaving both hands free for diapering. Forget whips, butt plugs, and nipple clamps: those BDSM people could make a fortune selling this invention online.

November 23, 2001

My first copy of *Parents* magazine arrived this week, and I finally got the courage to open it. I landed on a section called "It Worked for Me! Parents share their tried-and-true tips." This was the tip:

Celebrating Color: Every week, my 2-year-old daughter and I choose a new color to celebrate. We paint pictures, model clay, and eat foods all of the same color. Then we end the week with a

fun activity like a scavenger hunt. By finding objects that match our color, my daughter can show off what she's learned!
> —Shay Hess; LaGrange, Ga.

Who *are* these people? What human being actually has the time, not to mention the inclination, to color-code her food? Does Shay Hess think her daughter is going to make it to high school without knowing colors? *"What is this thing 'orange' of which you speak?"*

In women's magazines advertisers and readers have a tacit agreement: we will convince you that you have a genuine problem that can be helped with one of our products, and in exchange you will buy this product with the knowledge that you are not vain or greedy or bored but simply an intelligent person coming up with clever solutions to life's difficulties. The contract between advertisers and readers of parenting magazines is similar and even more ingenious: we will justify your desire to buy a lot of crap for your children by explaining that crap's sound educational value. On the one hand, you could hang some bright shiny objects over your kid's crib. *Or* you can spend fifty bucks on some *professionally approved, developmentally appropriate* bright shiny object that whirs and play Mozart.

Deep breaths. If I just accept the fact that magazines exist to fuel our inadequacies, I will be fine. And I think I'll

start color-coding Henry and Gus's food. It will be nice to
know what my children will talk about in therapy when
they are adults.

November 25, 2001
The boys celebrated their two-month birthday today. Here
is what Gus has learned in two months: how to miss the
burp cloth entirely when he throws up, despite the fact that
I hover in front of his face like Domenik Hasek trying to
block a wet, sticky puck. And here's what Henry's learned:
that a blood-curdling shriek, followed by deathly silence, is
enough to make a person rocket to his side. At which point I
am greeted by a small person with a beatific smile, not the
glassy-eyed corpse I'm expecting.

They went for their two-month checkups and eye tests—
including one test for Henry which involved dilating the
pupils, then holding the eyes open with little *Clockwork
Orange*-like prong devices and having lights shone into
them. They were brave. It's heartening to see how they go
from sixty-to-zero—heartrending sobs to silence—merely
by my picking them up. I am a superhero whose amazing
Cuddling Powers stop crying jags in their tracks! I am the
envy of all mortals! Fear me!

December 1, 2001

As I peck away at my computer this afternoon, Henry and Augustus lie on my bed, wriggling contentedly and digesting their bottles. It's a pleasure to contemplate their peaceful consanguinity, two brothers already enjoying their shared time together.

Then the tell-tale *horrrk*. Gus projectile vomits onto Henry, and there is this ever-so-brief delay while the boy who hates the slightest bit of dirt processes the information that he is soaked in someone else's spew.

Then Henry's piercing shrieks. Then Gus's startled wailing.

What separates bliss and hell when you've got small children: about ten seconds.

December 3, 2001

Nauseous and panicked and bargaining with God. One of Gus's newborn screening blood tests came back saying he has mildly elevated levels of a particular amino acid. This test means one of two things: a) nothing, or b) a horrible genetic disease that will kill or retard him. The disease is called homocystinuria, and it's a genetic tendency to have dangerously high levels of the amino acid homocysteine build up in the blood, resulting in premature hardening of the arteries and various life-threatening neurological conditions. It is incurable and terrifying.

I call my friend Steven, the doctor. I'm told Steven has a day job where he cures people, but since I've had Henry and Gus I'm pretty sure his main job is shouting at me over the phone, *"For God's sake, it's nothing!"* Today Steven tells me it's very common to have false positives on the test. I don't care if he's lying. I love Steven.

When the pediatrician calls and tells me Gus will have to be retested, I believe her voice belies her words. Her words are matter-of-fact: "I've never seen anyone with just a slight elevation have this disease." However, her tiny, sad little voice says to me, *"Not only does your child have this disease; this is the first of many you'll be coping with. Prepare to lose him from a stroke at the age of ten. But before he has the stroke, he'll be mentally incapacitated, so the stroke will come as a relief."*

How could Gus have this rare recessive-gene disease, given how disparate John's and my gene pools are? Me with genes from Russia and Italy, John a Celt—it's not like we're first cousins.

John is in England. I don't want to mention this to him, because the man who was trying to convince me that our other son had cri du chat syndrome is unlikely to be reassuring. (Never mind that I'd had amniocentesis and that this is one of the conditions you test for: John was convinced that because of the E.T.-like shape of his eyes and his odd little mewling cry, Henry had a chromosome defect that leads to mental retardation.) Plus there is the possibility that a conversation about this will allow him to turn to his usual refrain: *"If you had only eaten normally during your pregnancy..."*

Before the scheduled blood test I had a lunch date with an editor I barely knew, so I didn't want to cancel. Nor did I want to say what was bothering me. So I drank steadily throughout lunch, and by the time I got to the blood lab I was crying and exuding gin fumes. Gus had to be poked five times before they could fit the needle into his tiny vein. It was the only time I wished I was breast-feeding, so I could pass along the benefits of my soothing boozathon to him.

The doctor promises results tomorrow.

December 4, 2001
No results.

December 5, 2001
No results.

December 6, 2001
No results, and now the doctor tells me this could take a couple of *weeks.*

John doesn't come back from England for another five days. How does he manage to time his visits to avoid the moments when I'm in a state of panic?

December 14, 2001
They lost the test.

December 15, 2001
They found the test; it had been shipped to the wrong lab. I
heard two of the happiest words in the English language:
false positive. Steven the doctor explained what's happened:
Gus has probably inherited one copy of the bad gene, which
means he'd be well-advised to take vitamin B supplements,
to not smoke, and to exercise to avoid arterial plaque in his
fifties or sixties. What it does *not* mean is a stroke and
consequent mental retardation in childhood. This particular
gene—which allows for the buildup of homocysteine in the
blood, and subsequent arterial plaque issues—is five times
more common among Celts than among the rest of the
population. So I can blame John. Excellent.

I figure by the time Henry and Gus are five they can be
snorting Ajax and I won't care, because I'll have used up my
lifetime supply of anxiety in their first year.

I trace Augustus's furrowed little brow with my
fingertips. Isn't it strange that I should have been given the
most beautiful boy in the world?

December 16, 2001

John has said little about the medical scare, but he's been hovering over Gus since he returned from England. He spends a long time staring at him but is still reluctant to pick him up. Half the time I am loving John for bestowing on me these little messiahs; the other half I am in a homicidal rage because he is hardly ever around. He has more or less absented himself, with the excuse that it is uncomfortable living in my shoebox apartment with Yvonne perched in the living room. So he visits us to stare at the children and go to the gym.

Meanwhile, I've done nothing all day but ping-pong between these two babies. Oh! Look how cute he is, let me get the camera! Oh, now he's crying, but the other one is so cute, wait, let me focus! Oh, you need to be changed, come over here—no, wait, you need your bottle, let me put you down and ... OK, you've conked out but now *you* need the bottle? But you just had eight ounces, I can't give you any more ... OK, take the pacifier! No, don't spit it out. Wait, I just need to ... and then I look up and *seven hours have gone by.*

What's unsettling about babies is change, constant and unrelenting. I hate change. Change means never being prepared, because one doesn't know what a baby can do from one day to the next. Today Henry was resting comfortably on my bed, the dog snoozing on *his* bed just below. That's fine. Henry can't roll over. *Or can he?*

The next thing I know I hear a squeak, I look over, and Henry's lying face down on the dog, whimpering. The dog has his usual expression on his face—*Buh?*—but can't be bothered to move. I curse myself; I should have known this could happen. Bad mother. But good dog!

December 17, 2001

Last night I asked Yvonne if she ever disliked a child she was taking care of. "Sometimes the devil wants you to be defeated, so you have to defeat him," she said.

December 18, 2001

John and I left the kids at home and went to the Christmas party of our friends in Norwalk: glazed ham, biscuits, baked apples, a blazing fire, antique decorations on the Christmas tree; the pine-needles-and-cinnamon scent of a life well lived. Cornelia, one of the finest editors in the business, and her attorney husband, Edgar, are some of my favorite humans, though among their old-money, painfully Episcopalian crowd I always feel a little conspicuous: *"Hey, who let the Jew in?"* Theirs is the life John craves, among the old colonials and khakis dating back to St. Bernard's and oak furniture with a patina that only comes from being

passed through generations. "Wouldn't you like to live in
Norwalk someday?" he asks, as we hurry through the
whirling snow flurries that the ghost of Charles Dickens has
thoughtfully provided for the evening.

I'm never sure. A life so gentle and rich. But then I think
too of their only son, a brilliant and sweet boy who has spent
most of his life in and out of institutions. Voices that would
not let him rest, that compelled him to tear the flesh from
his own body. Finally they found the medication to quell
the voices. He is getting his Ph.D. in mathematics now; he
is at the top of his class. But he'll never be able to live alone,
and his parents will never be entirely free from the thought,
"What happens when we're gone?"

There is no perfect life, not even here. No amount of
privilege can protect you from a broken child.

December 19, 2001
Every morning at 8:15 I get the phone call: "What are the
babies doing?" The truthful answer to my mother's eager
question—eating, sleeping, shitting—is not all that
satisfying, which is how I have claimed for Henry and Gus
nuances of personality to which only a nineteenth-century
Russian novelist could do justice. A cock of the head, a
squint of the eye can open up doors to the future. The way
Augustus stretches his delicate, unusually long fingers:

surely that spread augurs an eleven-note reach! And the astounding thing is, my mother will listen to me. Not only listen, but listen as if she were Frodo and I were Gandalf revealing the secret of the Ring.

"My arms always ached for a baby," my mother has said. "When someone handed me their child, I felt like they were doing me such a favor." My mother wanted to have a gaggle of children, but she could only have me. When I was six months old, her mother and friends had to strong-arm her back to work: *"You didn't go to medical school so you could sit home with a baby all day."* Her waiting room was always stuffed with exasperated patients, because whenever children came to see her, she would stop what she was doing and show them their X rays: "Look, here's your heart, and those cloudy shadows over there are your lungs!" They didn't find another radiologist, however. She was much loved. They'd rather wait for her.

Twelve years ago my mother, tiny and fat, had a stroke. Although her intelligence was unaffected, she stopped practicing. "What if I only *think* I'm fine ... what if I miss something?" she says. She misses work so much. I've had her rip X rays out of my hands when a friend's sent them to her for a second opinion. The lasting effect of her stroke has been poor balance and weakness on her right side. She doesn't trust herself to hold Henry and Gus. When she

95

visits, she watches from a distance, smiling happily and shaking slightly. I imagine her arms still ache.

When I get the morning phone call and tell her Gus smiled, I can tell she's not even *thinking,* "It's just gas."

December 23, 2001

Brunch today with Steven, Cynthia, and their three kids while Henry and Gus slept peacefully in their stroller. At the end of the meal Jeffrey, their eleven-year-old, turned to me and said, "Are those your children? Wow. I thought you were just baby-sitting."

Even an eleven-year-old can sense I have no business having children.

December 25, 2001

I almost decided against Christmas. There is no place in this apartment for a tree, even the most sad, spindly Charlie Brown tree left in the lot on Christmas Eve. But I needed those baby/tree photos, had to have them, even if the tree wasn't my own. So I packed John, the dog, and the boys in their matching polar bear sweaters (just this one time I'd make with the matching clothing, I told myself) into the Jeep, and we headed to my cousin Amy's in Westchester. Fifteen years from now I'll tell them it was their tree, the first I'd decorated especially for them. If they're as observant about photos as I am, they'll never notice the difference.

Nobody loves a beautiful tree better than a bunch of Scarsdale Jews, and my cousin really outdid herself. All the kids got a huge haul; it looked like Toys "R" Us ralphed in her living room. My aunt Alberta in particular was generous, though I think she shopped for baby clothes in *Soldier of Fortune* magazine: she managed to find itsy bitsy flak jackets for Henry and Gus, with teeny zippered compartments. What are they going to hold in there, pacifiers? But at any rate, H & G were mauled by adults and children all day and hardly uttered a peep. Henry actually enjoyed being passed around. Gus had a look on his face that was a little more long-suffering, but I told him I was proud of him as I rescued him from Ava, my cousin's five-year-old, and he burped appreciatively in my face.

We visited Uncle Albert in the nursing home, where we are praying his stay is temporary. Got some great pictures of him holding Henry and Gus. We met Sarah, the director of rehab, a lovely fortyish woman with a Dorothy Hamill bob and deep blue eyes that slant down at the corners. Slanting-down eyes invariably make a face kindly, and a little sad. She is unusually attentive to my seventy-six-year-old uncle. I've heard she loves classical music, and although he can't talk, my uncle loves to teach. He's always mentored others. They seem to spend many hours together. She spent a lot of time massaging his paralyzed arm. *A lot* of time.

On the ride home John and I, having been unable to sit down and have a proper conversation with anyone at Christmas dinner, squabbled over nothing until all petty subjects were exhausted and we fell back on silence. As we wove our way down the Saw Mill River Parkway, I thought about what the holidays would have been like with Benjamin. Benjamin was the Orthodox Jewish Englishman I was scheduled to marry before John. Slim and neat, with perfect olive skin, beautiful seal eyes, and a nose so large one half expected him to remove it—*haha! Joke nose!*— Benjamin was often not so very happy with his Jewish but half-Italian, holiday-loving fiancée. I was assimilated enough to take pleasure in the icicle-festooned Christmas trees and the cute pastel bunnies at Easter, if not in the birth and the resurrection itself. I listened to endless lectures about the dangers of my carelessness, the confusion it would cause our future children, though a request for fellatio was generally followed by a request that I kiss the *Chumash,* so Benjamin was not without his own contradictions. I adored and disliked him in equal measure, thought him a charming hypocrite, and when he infuriated me, which was often, I rejoiced in sneaking into his kitchen and rubbing his milk and meat dishes together.

Still, I would have happily married him, would have tried very hard to celebrate the Sabbath and to bake hamantaschen on Purim and not to lift a pen on Saturdays, if we had not had the following prenuptial conversation. He had announced we would have as many children as we could afford, because it was our duty as Jews to repopulate the world with people of our intelligence and breeding. "What if one of your children married someone who wasn't Jewish?" I asked absentmindedly, expecting to hear a lecture about how horrible that would be, but obviously one accepts one's children for who they are and what they want.

"Well, of course that child would be dead to me," he said.

"Oh, c'mon," I replied. "You're kidding, right?" Before we met, Benjamin had been engaged to an Episcopalian.

"No, I am not kidding," he said, his perfect skin blotching a little. "I would forget I ever knew him."

My poor parents. They had already spent thousands to reserve the banquet hall.

As I settled Henry and Gus into their cribs tonight, I asked myself what it would take for me to be so disappointed I would be able to consider them dead. Rape? Murder? I could turn them in, but I'd still visit them at Sing Sing. Maybe there's something they could do, I don't know. But whatever it is, I know it isn't choosing the wrong person to love.

December 31, 2001

I've no idea how to stay married. In fact, I wonder how anyone stays married when they have children.

I got the familiar speech this afternoon: "I never made a secret of how I felt about children. But now you've got your children, you should be happy," and I found myself crying on the streets of Manhattan as I haven't since I was actively dating and therefore sobbing about eighty percent of the time. Only now I'm forty and weeping and pathetic, instead of twenty-two and weeping and interesting. I felt I could have sat in a pile of breadcrumbs, and even the pigeons would have passed me by.

When I was twenty-two I felt sorry for myself. At forty I feel sorry for Henry and Gus. What would it be like for them without a father? If we separate, I could always tell them he's dead, because by the time they're aware enough to ask the question, he might be. All I wanted was a family. How conventional, how bourgeois! But when you can't make a person happy no matter how hard you try, why bother?

Well, I still want one, and I'm going to have one, one way or the other. If John doesn't want to be in it, I'll find someone who does.

At least I have a New Year's resolution.

January 2, 2002

OK, this probably isn't such a good resolution; I should go back to just trying to get a flatter stomach. Still, Match.com has become such a huge universe. Surely there are thousands of men, or hundreds, or one, who would like to strike up a friendship with a slovenly middle-aged mother of three-month-olds "who owns several apartments in New York"—there, I just widened my audience. "Must enjoy company of needy overweight shedding odoriferous dog"—that narrows it a bit—"and quickies at four in the afternoon"—wider—"preferably in your enormous corner office." Well, there's got to be something in it for me.

Contemplating what it would be like to put my picture up on Match.com, it's hard to narrow down exactly which is *the* most irksome thing about motherhood at this point. Is it the physical exhaustion, the boredom in the playground after five minutes? Is it the tragedy of having evicted myself from the Garden of Eden that was my thirties as I approached the pinnacle of freedom and career? Or is it simply the permanent circles under my eyes, the nasolabial grooves carved into my face as on one of those wooden-Indian statues, and the ineluctable pull of gravity everywhere that nothing short of Demi Moore-esque plastic surgery efforts can cure?

I lose my courage to post an ad before the day is through, but I did check up on matches in my area and managed to thoroughly depress myself. If I plug in search terms that include men between the ages of thirty-five and fifty-five in a five-mile radius from my apartment (don't love to travel), Match.com comes back with 250 possible matches. When I key in the words "loves children" I get six. Of those six, several look like they love children in a very special way I didn't intend.

January 5, 2002

Today got a crib mobile that promises to improve baby's cognitive and spatial skills, but in reality improves a mother's cognitive and spatial skills by forcing her to spend three hours piecing it together. After I finally get this sucker to belt out its tinny Bach, Mozart, and Beethoven while frogs whirl overhead, I notice the directions say, "Not to be used for babies over five months." Apparently, once they can reach up and grab it, they can get entangled in it and it becomes a strangling hazard. I am so glad I'm fifty dollars poorer and three hours closer to death so that my children can hear "Ode to Joy" played on a fifty-cent microchip instead of the five-hundred-dollar CD player that's also next to their crib.

January 15, 2002

This is the day I've been dreading for weeks. Yvonne has left. Because I'm such a weenie about getting sleep, I have kept her here, living on my couch, for more than three months. CEOs of Fortune 500 companies have not kept a baby nurse as long as I have. But now the babies are sleeping through the night and I have no more excuses. My days of pretending I'm Madonna, able to afford $250 a day for a twenty-four-hour nurse, are over. And it's not like I even took much advantage of having all that help. Like an idiot I rang in the New Year eating Macarena almonds and drinking Veuve Clicquot at home—with Yvonne. We spent the evening being enthusiastic spectators at the baby rollover Olympics, which consisted of my placing Henry on his stomach and cheering when he managed to flip over. I love when they start flipping like little pancakes. They look so surprised every time. The expression on their faces is, "Oh my God, if I can do that, what else can I do? *Maybe I can levitate.*"

Anyway, Yvonne told me she was getting me the perfect nanny. "My sister will be coming here," she said firmly. I nodded. I'm sure there are some women who at that moment would have said, "Thanks so much, but I'd prefer to find my own nanny." I am not one of them. Generally I'm so intimidated by anyone who has the guts to ask me for

work that I give it to them. I should just be grateful
Yvonne's sister was not Susan Smith, because she'd probably
be my nanny right now.

January 16, 2002
Orma arrived. She is tall and powerfully built like her sister.
Most of the time her face is plain and impassive. But when
she smiles, she lights up from the inside. She has said
nothing to me, but for the past six hours she has been
upstairs, chattering to Henry and Gus. At the end of the day
she turned to me and said, "You have to take the time to get
to know them." Then she turned and walked away.

Okeydokey then! This should work out just fine. And if it
doesn't, you still have a job, because *you scare the shit out of me.*

January 18, 2002
It's too soon to be cocky about this, but at least there's one
lasting legacy of the Yvonne months. It seems her babies-
that-sleep-through-the-night fairy dust has lasted; they're
still sleeping, even now that she's gone. Would I have rather
had a new car or sleeping infants? Surely that's worth the
$23,000 it cost to keep her here.

I'm going to a magazine party tonight, and before I leave
John asks me, for perhaps the seventeenth time, "Now, are
you sure their diapers are clean?" He has announced his

intention to make it through the first three years of their lives without ever changing a diaper, and so far he's been successful. On the other hand, I remind myself, I'd rather change ten diapers than face vomit, a bodily fluid he seems to have no problem with. So we've staked out our orifices and are sticking to them.

January 19, 2002

"You can't afford to have twins in New York City," my cousin Amy told me when she heard I was pregnant. "You're going to have to move to the suburbs." I was so irritated by this pronouncement that I decided then and there I would not move. Surely a little cutting back would enable me to stay here and live comfortably.

The sticker shock is only beginning to sink in. Here are just a few of the costs I have incurred since having Henry and Gus:

$370,000: the one-bedroom apartment I bought above the one I own so I have someplace to keep them

$100,000: approximately what the remodeling will cost to make the two apartments into one

$987 a month: the monthly maintenance on that additional apartment

$600 a month: extra health insurance, on top of my
   regular health insurance, for a family plan

$20 x 2: the co-pays every time I take the two of them to
   the doctor, which I have to do a lot

$2400 a month: salary for Orma, who allows me to work
   so I can make the money for everything else

$500 every six weeks: formula

$150 a month: diapers

$40,000 a year for school: starting in two and a half years,
   if I stay in Manhattan and public schools continue to rot

a gazillion dollars a month for clothing, books, videos,
   and ugly chirping plastic toys

Most people assume none of this is a problem; I'm married
to a man twenty-five years older than I am. What idiot
would marry someone twenty-five years older who wasn't
wealthy just because she loved him?

This idiot.

Not surprisingly I am having panic attacks about work.
May never be able to concentrate on anything again, won't
be able to pay mortgage, children out on the street shaking
Styrofoam cups.

I shouldn't have confided this to John. He likes to tell the
kids stories, and today I hear him saying to Henry, "and
then we'll put you outside with a Styrofoam cup, and you

can collect money for your mother and me, because we're poor, you know. Quite poor!" At which point Henry goes from all smiles to puckered frown, and then he bawls. I admonish John, and a few minutes later he's telling the same story to Augustus, and this time *Gus* bursts into tears.

John is quietly happy. "I feel a sense of artistic integrity," he says. "My voice must create an atmosphere."

January 20, 2002

I took the boys to the doctor's yesterday for shots, weighing, etc. Henry is still clueless: he goes into the doc's office all smiles and gets this look of shock and betrayal on his face when the needle goes in. (Mark the agent has created a sniglet for this moment, the time lapse between the moment babies get a shot and the moment they react. There's the hiatus, then the crying: it's a criatus!) Gus, on the other hand, only has to see Nurse Doris—who's given him these shots a number of times now—to dissolve into piteous wailing, which doesn't let up until the injections are over. Then he collapses in a damp, gasping heap in my arms. Orma gets so upset when she sees Henry and Gus carrying on she has to leave the room. Still, I have to love her. Instead of saying what I was thinking—"Oh for God's sake, don't be such a little chicken!" she said, "Augustus is so sensitive and intelligent! He knew what was coming!"

Gus is not yet on the charts for his weight and is only at five percent for height, but given his weight at birth, that's not unusual. I'm trying not to freak out because, after weighing and measuring Henry yesterday, we discovered he's in the fiftieth percentile for weight—huge, for a kid who started life at three pounds—and fifth percentile for height. Translation: he is short and fat. Not to mention bald. Oh, and his head is in the ninety-fifth percentile. Short, fat, bald and a craniac. His neck has all but disappeared. John thinks it's a Celtic trait: his neck is being pushed down into his torso through the sheer weight of his despair.

January 21, 2002

Henry is a whining, gushing fountain of drool. I say it's the shots and the teething; John says it's his innate evil nature.

On days like this it's not infanticide that amazes me. It's the converse miracle—that more people don't kill their children. Today I decided I would do the world a favor and get rid of this mewling, shitting, sweaty, spotty-faced wretch. I could save civilization from these headlines:

Boy, 10, Steals American Constitution, Sets It On Fire
Manhattan Prep School Youngster, Bald, Leads Wilding
Massive Slaying of Puppies At ASPCA By Marauding 12-

*Year-Old Holds No Surprises For Friends And Family:
"He Was Always A Loner"*

To ease his discomfort, I start with a frozen bagel, progress
to a teething ring filled with water, and end up dipping a
pacifier repeatedly into John's single malt. Guess which
method worked? Eventually he was cooing. Then he passed
out. Next stop: Valium drip until puberty.

January 22, 2002
Augustus woke up at 4 A.M. sobbing with another one of his
bad dreams. But a quick pat on the back puts him back to
sleep. Doctors say babies don't have nightmares until
they're two. But that's because they can *ask* a two-year-old.
Who can ask a four-month-old? And what is a bad dream
for a baby, anyway? Being hungry, being wet, being left
alone . . . for Gus, it's probably a world without pacifiers.

The mind of a baby: the final frontier.

Later this afternoon, to irritate John I showed him what
happens when I play "The Man That Got Away" for Henry
and Gus. By the time Judy Garland gets to *"No more his eager
call/The writing's on the wall,"* Gus's lower lip is trembling,
and in a few seconds he's heaving great sobs. "Look!" I say.
"He's a Friend of Dorothy!"

Secretly, I do wonder why more women don't actively hope to have a gay son. I do. Not both of them, because that would be a bit much; plus I want grandchildren (should I live so long). But if one were gay? Someone who probably would have better taste than I do, perhaps a sense of style, liked to cook, might devote his life to interesting work instead of having a family, would introduce me to his cool friends? What's not to like?

All stereotypes, I know, guaranteeing me equal amounts of hate mail from both Christian fundamentalists *and* the Lambda League. Still, there's one stereotype that does hold true for virtually every gay man I know: they're close to their mothers.

Of course, wishing for a gay son out loud probably guarantees both Henry and Gus will be straight. Not that there's anything wrong with that.

February 4, 2002, A.M.
Henry just ate rice cereal thickened with formula for the first time. I think he saw God. From the look in his eyes, one could hear the harps and heavenly choir. "This boy likes his food," Orma exclaimed enthusiastically.

P.M.

Now I realize what Henry's look means. It translates to "Oh, boy! Now I can *really* throw up!"

February 5, 2002

This morning I was reminded quite forcefully of the difference between a baby who only drinks milk and a baby who's eating solid food. Solid food is where the serpent enters Eden, from the nasty-diaper point of view.

February 6, 2002

It's sad that I'm going to have to give them away. They don't have that fire in the belly. They're not performers. I had been telling a friend how Augustus beamed and clasped his hands when I sang him show tunes, and she actually traveled from the Upper West Side to witness this phenomenon. As soon as she arrived, Henry passed out and Augustus shrieked for an hour. I think I could run one of those "don't let this happen to you" programs for teenagers thinking of having children. All they have to do is visit me around dinner time: kids screaming, take-out Chinese swimming in oil, dog nudging my leg for attention, all in an apartment the size and charm level of an NYU student dorm. I give squalor a bad name.

Dropping into bed exhausted, I realized I should have gone with my original plan and adopted a girl from China. Not only would she be beautiful (my theory about overpopulation in China: of course there are too many, they can't help themselves, they make the cutest babies), she'd probably be playing violin by now.

February 14, 2002

Got my first Valentine's Day gift from Henry and Gus—a ribbon that reads "World's Best Mom." John got his first gift from them too (a gift, I hasten to add, he bought for himself). His ribbon says "Older than God." On the envelope he'd written "Happy whatever—enjoy it while you can, it's nearly over," and on the back of the ribbon, "To Crinkly, from the Boys."

John was actually very sweet on Valentine's Day, and by "sweet" I mean "didn't complain too much." But he went home at nine, despite the fact that Monty had diarrhea. I knew what this meant: essentially, I'd find myself walking the streets at three in the morning with an incontinent golden retriever. I was sure the police were on the way to my empty apartment, where, upon my return, I'd be arrested for child neglect. As I walked the block, thinking of the boys alone upstairs (*"Officer, it was either leave them alone for five minutes or ruin a ten-thousand-dollar Persian carpet"*), I thought of that article I'd read recently in the *National Enquirer* about autocombustion. Apparently, under certain circumstances, a person could heat up and burst into flames. Usually the flames start in the head. Henry and Gus always have hot heads. By 3:10 A.M. I am on the street shivering, the dog shooting liquid feces, knowing that I am going to be arrested not only for child abuse but also for arson, when my sons' heads combust and burn down the building.

I come back to find Gus cooing in the dark. I pick him up and feel his head and it is hot. But it is still attached to his body. I feed the dog two Imodium wrapped in cheese and think about the many Valentine's Days when John and I and a bottle of Krug went to a country bed-and-breakfast and didn't emerge from the room until February 16.

February 22, 2002

I've never been one to spend much time decoding other people's clothing, but I have to wonder: why have so many people given my sons outfits with trucks on them? Why, indeed, are trucks a major motif in boys' clothing? Do parents buy this stuff for their own children? *"Why yes, it's my fondest wish that my son grow up to drive a Bigfoot."* On girls, sure, you see flowers, but you also occasionally see flowers on grown women. I don't recall seeing too many Fortune 500 chairmen with eighteen-wheelers sewed onto their lapels.

February 23, 2002

My friend Nigella's in town; she was on Regis and Kelly
yesterday, so I had to call and personally apologize for
American morning television. We went out to eat at Lupa's.
Given her growing fame in this country as a TV chef it's always
fun going out with her, because the chef of the restaurant
greets us and gives us little treats. Later she came over and met
the babies—inhaled them really: "Oh, I remember this smell,"
she said. "It's the smell of wild mushrooms."

February 25, 2002

Nancy keeps telling me I'm the most relaxed new mother
she's ever seen. Nancy is one of the most loving, thoughtful
women I know, and also a bit of a hypochondriac. So I'm
pretty sure "relaxed" is her code for "You're too stupid to
know how much there is to worry about." And perhaps it is
true that I should have reacted more quickly when Henry
took the dog's slimy tennis ball and put it in his mouth. But
as usual I thought, "Well, that's why we have a liver."

What Nancy doesn't understand is that I'm not so much
relaxed as resigned to the inevitable. It's a little like saying
Beth in *Little Women* was relaxed: no, not really, but she
knew it was her duty as an angelic child and a narrative
device to shuffle off this mortal coil. So why fight it? When
you're twenty-five, you still think so much is in your

control. By the time you hit forty, you realize that if it's meant for your child to contract mad cow disease because you didn't wash the bottle's nipples in hot enough water, well then so be it. Not that you're blithely ignorant of danger, not that you don't take precautions, but you also pick your battles against the universe. The fact is there is much danger in the world, yet the vast majority of children survive.

By the end of most days I'm thinking, "Wow, they're still here. Cool."

February 28, 2002

Forget everything I just said. Never relax.

The last words I heard before he tumbled down the stairs were "Fine. He's playing by himself." That was in answer to my question to John, "How's Henry?" I will always see my small and chubulous son rolling down, down, like the barrel he resembles; I'll hear the *thud-thud-thud* of his head smacking the stairs; I will relive this scene, as in a Peckinpah movie, in slo-mo. He doesn't know how to crawl yet. Who knew a baby could roll that quickly?

I grab him. He screams and clutches me. John grabs him. I grab him back. John and I are both shouting at each other, *"I thought you were watching him!"* Henry's forehead turns pink. I check the arms and legs, as John looks up head injuries in the Merck manual. I don't know why I'm checking to see if his pupils are pinpoints, but I know if they are, it's bad. They're not. John croons to him, and he stops whimpering and smiles. Then he starts to cry again. But then, of course, it's 6 P.M.—dinnertime.

A bottle and a half later he's snoring, and I'm debating the emergency room. To go or not to go? If I call the litigation-wary pediatrician, she'll tell me to go. I don't call. If I wake him up to go to the emergency room, we'll be there half the night getting CAT scans. I don't go.

Is he still breathing?

7:20 Still breathing.

7:30 Still breathing.

7:45 He draws breath.

8:00 Alive.

8:05 Still here. I'm not going to check again until 9.

8:25 That was pretty good. And he's still here. He's sleeping deeply. But is he sleeping *too* deeply?

9:00 He's starting his nightly rotation. Normally in the course of a night he turns around in a complete circle. Right now he's at 45 degrees. In a half-hour he should be at 180 degrees.

10:00 180 degrees. Limbs still working.

11:00 Sleeping. Coma?

We were up about every thirty minutes; we might as well have gone to the hospital and sat there all night with the knife and gunshot wounds. But at least *he* slept. This morning: walloped down his usual bottles and peach goop; not even a bump or a swelling. I've spent the last nine years watching my cousin Amy drag her kids to the ER every time they fell down, and I didn't want to overreact. Still, John and I will spend the next twenty years wondering, every time Henry does something stupid, *"Was it the stairs?"*

John is out buying a baby gate. I am very tired.

March 1, 2002

Still shattered from yesterday. Of course my first thought was for Henry's safety. But my second thought was a little less altruistic: *"Oh my God, Orma must never find out this happened."* As it is she calls me on her days off to see how the children are doing. She always sounds a little surprised to hear they're still alive.

This afternoon she asked me about the baby gate: why did we get one at this particular time? Her eyes narrowed. I said nothing.

March 6, 2002

These no-necks, they are scary. They look fragile. They act like disinterested parties to their own personal hygiene—dressing, diapering, wiping the face. They could care less. They're unhelpful. But they work very, very hard. They stare & think & stare & ponder & stare until they cannot keep their eyes open any longer. And think of the indignities. Can you imagine having someone pick you up and position you any way they damn well please? And then, once they've got you where they want you, they put a funny hat and sunglasses on you.

Henry and Gus are rather solemn (See: husband's morose DNA), and being silly doesn't come naturally to me, so it's fun when I can finally figure out how to make them laugh. But the same things never work on both of them. Henry's a slave to peekaboo: I hide my face, uncover it . . . gales of laughter. I do that to Gus and he just looks at me quizzically, like, "Um, can I help you? One second you're not here, the next second you're here . . . is there some confusion I can clear up?"

But when the baby stuff is good, it's good. Henry is sitting in my lap right now, drinking me in with those huge gray storm-cloud eyes. I may be a plump middle-aged woman to the rest of the world, but to Henry I am Parvati, Hindu goddess of love. This is only right. It's my duty to encourage him in his worship of women.

I tried very hard to get good photos of them today, but every time I try, they do their Sean Penn imitations: bonny smiles until I get the camera focused, then hands in front of their eyes, with pained expressions that say, *"Can't a man just live his life?"*

March 7, 2002

Because John and I still have separate apartments, and because he wakes up in the middle of the night and can't get back to sleep when Gus and Henry cry, he comes down here for nookie and then goes home.

On the one hand, it's good we actually do get to have sex now and then, because after eleven years I still think everything about him is delicious. My older friends with new babies say I shouldn't complain. Many are going through what my friend Marjorie calls the New Virginity, the return to an adolescent state of hormonal derangement and body-image worry combined with middle-aged exhaustion. Add to it the overlay of spousal ambivalence—the man's mental neutering of his wife, who is now supposed to be a mommy and not a lust object—and it's astounding anyone ever gets a chance to be pregnant a second time.

On the other hand, I'm beginning to feel like he should leave a C-note on the nightstand.

March 8, 2002

Henry tried to kiss me today. He got this fierce look of concentration on his face, then made lips like a sea bass and with one desperate lunge banged his entire head into my cheek. He missed my lips and gave me a bruise, but the good intentions were there.

March 10, 2002

Fifteen years ago I was talking to the friend of a Very Famous Writer, known for her novels about sex, and the friend told me how the writer had *kvelled* over her newborn daughter. "Look at that pussy," the Famous Writer said. "Isn't it a beautiful pussy?" Fifteen years ago I found that story degenerate. I thought perhaps FW should to go jail. Now I sit around and admire my boys' dicks.

Sometimes I think I should go to jail for just thinking about it. But more often I think, "Now I get it." FW couldn't help but cherish every particle of her daughter. I mean, there they are, all these parts, more exquisite than they'll ever be again in a human's lifetime. And the parts do just what they're supposed to do. The skin cells multiply wildly, and the baby grows. The baby fills his pants, and you know his intestines are doing their job, absorbing what they need for life and getting rid of the rest. Their penises allow them to pass urine, just as God or Nature intended. Someday those penises will give them much happiness. Now I understand Alexander Portnoy's mother too. Philip Roth made her into a monster of obtrusiveness, with an unwholesome interest in her son's eating habits and bowel movements and *schlong*. But the truth is, poor Sophie Portnoy just lost track of time. She looked at a man and saw a baby. And if her son was a baby, she was a pretty young thing too. How could Sophie Portnoy help herself? How can any of us?

I'll never force Henry and Gus to talk about their bodies or sex or anything of the sort when they're older; I won't embarrass them like Sophie. The minute they want their privacy, they've got it, and I will be quite happy never to see them naked again. But for now, while they're babies, I will take a sensual pleasure in every beautiful inch.

Which I hope for their sakes turns into eight inches. But then I was always a size queen.

March 13, 2002

What were we fighting about? Does it matter? It was the fight of weariness, when the most hateful thing about the person you love is that you know, as sure as eggs is eggs, the next tedious complaint that's going to come out of his mouth. A uniquely unpleasant performance artist said her greatest fear was "being held a captive by niceness," and for once in my entirely too pleasant life I didn't want to be niceness's slave. I know I shouldn't have yelled, particularly not at the gallery opening. But the fourth glass of cheap white wine sent me over the edge. *"We have the world's most perfect children and you don't appreciate them,"* I cried, as the Dolce & Gabbana–clad crowd backed away slowly, honoring the crazy-person force field I seem to create every time I step out of the house with my husband.

Back home at midnight, I tried to stop myself. But the need to Google was stronger than I was.

Mason: whatever happened to him? I loved him in the way you could only love someone you really knew nothing about. He was large-boned and gangly, with black hair and white skin that was almost translucent; his cheeks were hollow in a consumptive, romantic way. He was a mathematician. He wore no underwear. He was the first. I hold him personally responsible for some of the worst prose of my life.

I saw Mason today, probably for the last time. If I could only capture now, forever, the beauty of his pallor, the strange tension between the gawky boy-man frame, the huge bones barely covered by the luminescent flesh—and the essential feline grace. Strange how the dark, owlish horn-rimmed glasses made him look even younger, even more perplexing, even more distant. I leave Mason behind as I leave Wesleyan—with a certain amount of

tenderness despite it all. Despite the pettiness, and the
preposterousness, the injustice of both. Neither helped me when I
needed help. Both have drained me, shaped me. Hurt me in ways
they were unaware of. Mason, I can write it now, four years
after the fact, after all the people in between who have been
better, far better—that I loved you, and I know you were a
bastard, and still I loved you. Or, I should say, the ghost of
you, for you were never as I saw you then.

It goes on like this, for pages. I've often thought I should
enter my journal about Mason in the Bulwer-Lytton Bad
Writing contest. At the very least, I feel these letters should
be taught in a college journalism course, so that the
professor could then say to his students, "See? You can be
this bad at twenty, and still grow up to make a living as a
writer." I would be an inspiration.

Mason disliked his mother specifically and women
generally, so I guess it wasn't too surprising to see him, now
in his forties, still involved in a variety of singles groups. He
is now chipmunk-cheeked and still wearing the same horn-
rimmed glasses; he grins back at me from a Web site that is
all about mountaineering. By day he does something that
involves toxic waste. On weekends he leads snowshoeing
expeditions. So I can see that if we had stayed together, we
would have continued to have a lot in common.

Our children would be doing differential calculus at five, though.

March 15, 2002

Uncle Albert moved back to his Upper West Side studio apartment, which is in the same building as John's apartment. There is much arguing in the family over whether he really belongs there; he really can do nothing for himself and requires twenty-four-hour care. But this is where he wants to be, and no one wants to cross him. Friends drop by to visit. John says the most frequent visitor is Sarah, the lovely fresh-faced director of rehab from the nursing home. She seems to be taking a personal interest in his case.

Last night Uncle Albert asked John if he could score some Viagra.

March 17, 2002

I finally own the ugly-ass apartment above me. Actually, I've owned it for two months and have had to conclude that it is not going to magically fuse with the apartment I live in without some intervention on my part. Which means renovations. I haven't started to do anything yet, but I've hired the architect. Well, "hired" may be too strong a word. I brought a bottle of wine for my next-door neighbor George, who is an architect, and begged him to help me. He designs some of the chicest retail spaces in New York City, so this is like asking de Kooning to paint my bathroom. But I talked him into it. I figure that even though this job means nothing to him, he's got to do it well, seeing as how he lives next door and if his structural changes don't work out, my apartment caves in on his head.

The very word "renovation" fills me with cold dread. On the advice of my design-maven friends Casey and Randall, I went to Kohler.com and discovered a) the only bathroom I like would be perfect in an adobe cottage in New Mexico, not so very suitable for a New York City co-op, and b) it is possible to spend $1,400 on a faucet. And do you know how many kinds of faucets they have? They have 149, precisely 147 more than it takes to thrust me into a panic of indecision. *And that's just the faucet.* Do you have any idea how many towel racks exist in this universe?

But I must do something. I can't live like this anymore. Tonight I fell over the dog three times. Each time he yelped, then licked my foot. Thank God John still has his own apartment. What would life be like if I had to live with him too?

March 26, 2002

As I embark on my apartment makeover, I realize I have to do something to make over this body. I must be the only person in Manhattan to emerge svelte from pregnancy with twins, then proceed to eat myself up to the weight I should have been when I was six months pregnant. Why? Why?

Mucking about on the Internet, I think I may have found help: Strollercize! (Their motto: "Because a fit parent is more fit to parent.") Essentially you take your kid, strap him in a stroller, and wheel him around Central Park with other desperate mothers at top speed. *"Strollercize® works both the mind and body and in the first couple of classes it will be hard but then again . . . isn't motherhood! You will get it and you will use the system in your daily life."* I wonder how many of them are pushing twins. I wonder how many are pushing forty-one.

I sign up.

(I never make it to one class. Not one.)

March 28, 2002

Today I turned forty-one. I wasn't throwing up and I wasn't fighting with John, plus I have children. So it was a beautiful day.

March 30, 2002

Food poisoning. Fever, diarrhea, puking so severe I bled. As I lay in bed shivering, John stroked my head. "Don't you die and leave me with these two sodding kids and the bloody dog," he murmured.

April 13, 2002

My friend Marjorie tells me I have to get out more. She convinced me to come to her new mothers support group. Marjorie is a joiner. I am not.

As friends, Marjorie and I stare at each other cheerfully across an age divide. She's only seven years younger than I am, but that seven years is a huge chasm. It's more than a difference in earrings (mine) versus nose rings (hers), Bee Gees and Elvis Costello, Watergate and Contragate. It's the difference between coming of age in a recession, at a time of great disappointment in our leaders and heroes, and coming of age in a time of expansive optimism (even if, like Marjorie, you hated Reaganomics and all it stood for, you were still there at the party). She has a nostalgia for all the sisterhood-is-powerful stuff that only comes by not living through it. (Sisterhood *is* powerful, as long as you're not sitting in a circle yammering about it for four hours.)

Which is to say, Marjorie loves her new mothers support group and wanted me to love it too.

I lasted long enough to find out the names of the babies in the group:

Lion
Lola

Nevin (but with a Gaelic spelling, so it was Naomhan)
Diego
Lucas
Olivia
Maisy (2)
Nora
Talia
Tallulah
Ruby (2)
Zebulon

Can I bare my soul to a woman who named her child Zebulon? Where is the support group for mothers who named their children Jane, Susan, and Fred?

Before I fled I got to listen in on a conversation about breast-feeding. But not their babies. "My husband loves to drink my milk," says one woman. "It's always been his fantasy. He's had a lot more energy since he started, too." The woman with the newly energized husband is also a big believer in how breast milk is the only medication her daughter needs. The child recently had an eye infection. "I just put a few drops of my milk in there," she said. "Cleared it right up."

It must be nice to think your body is all-healing and all-powerful. Though there is a certain element of narcissism.

Even Marjorie was a bit startled. "What if you had a headache and I refused to give you aspirin?" Marjorie whispers to me. *"Sorry, you can't have aspirin, but I will lick you!"*

April 15, 2002
Period started today, which is a relief. One of the many annoyances of being a mother at this stage is that you're not quite as sure as you once were when your period will make its appearance, and since your mind is so often on things other than your own body, you're not always prepared. This month I swore I'd be ready, was indeed expecting it for days: bring on the deluge. Then, nothing. It takes the removal of Tampax and the wearing of beige shorts—not to mention the sudden chattiness of a neighbor who's never spoken to me in nine years—to get things going. She stops to admire my children. "So, do your parents live in New York?" she begins, as I realize a trickle of blood is about to course down my leg. I'm about to become a made-for-TV movie, *Carrie: The Menopause Years.* Yet there's a small part of me—a very small part, at that moment—who's relieved this is happening, relieved to have that not-as-perfectly-reliable-as-it-once-was-but-nevertheless-still-there reminder of what was, not what will be. Old I may be, but I'm still in the game.

April 16, 2002

Gus and Henry have synchronized their gums and decided to teethe simultaneously. For the past few nights they've been waking up, crying, at 4 A.M. It is only by attaching an IV drip of formula infused with tons of rice cereal that I managed last night to get them to sleep until 5:30. The dawn chorus of sparrows outside my window doesn't help. I have to live in Manhattan to be awakened at 4 every morning by *birds?*

During the day Henry and Gus sit there with their fists in mouths, eyes wide, gushing drool, with an expression on their faces that says, *"Make it stop."* When he woke up this morning, Henry was gnawing on the side of the crib like a beaver. I spend a good part of the day just dabbing at their mouths. I fantasize about stuffing their cheeks with cotton so they could a) perfect their Don Corleone imitations and b) stop being so damn moist.

Even with the teething and the saliva and the complaining though, sometimes I think John is warming to them. And why wouldn't he? At this point they just have to hear his voice coming in the door and they're practically barking like seals to get his attention.

April 17, 2002

Maybe picking a pediatrician because she has a beautiful name isn't such a great idea. But a few months ago I thought, "Catherine Deneuve: how can I go wrong?" (Catherine Deneuve is not, strictly speaking, her name. But would you like your pediatrician to hate you? Me neither.) And she is, in fact, lovely and thorough—maybe a little too thorough for someone like me who worries enough about health already. "You'll have to work with Gus on his eating problem," she says at his six-month checkup, where he weighed only nine pounds. "I want to see him in six weeks." OK, so at six months he doesn't like bananas or pears; I'm supposed to hire a team of specialists? Apparently I am.

Dr. Deneuve has referred me to an Early Intervention program for kids who have special needs. There might be many reasons. For Henry and Gus, being born premature at three pounds is reason enough. They have some catching up to do. I am a little nervous about all this—*my* children? special needs?—but I'm grateful. It is the first time in my life I've taken something free from the government.

And even a defensive mother could not fail to see that Augustus needs the therapy, not only because he's still smaller than a three-month-old and throws up any solid food, but because he's not the sociable creature Henry is. He has a way of averting his gaze from people when they try to engage him; he doesn't really love to be held; he can't stand loud noises; he's very, very good—*too* good. I'd been reading up on autism.

Naturally I'd voiced these concerns to the Early Intervention people, and they sent over an evaluator. She could see what I was talking about. Having been so tiny and premature at birth, he's still delayed physically, but she sort of scoffed at my autism theory. Not that you can really tell these things so early anyway, but I was told he was just doing typical preemie things, being a little overwhelmed by too much stimulus—lots of touch, lots of sound, intense eye contact. "You wouldn't have thought much about it if it weren't for Slim over here," she said, pointing to Henry. Henry, all nineteen pounds of him, had spent the entire time she was there trilling and gurgling and bada-badaing and essentially doing everything in his power to get her attention. Finally he just hurled himself in her arms like a human shot put.

This woman also made me feel better about Henry. I've been grateful he's caught up with other six-month-olds in most ways so quickly, but if he was so big why couldn't he sit up?

"Um, have you taken a good look at him?" she said. "He's totally top-heavy. It's gonna take him a while to balance all that weight." And it was true: like John, he's all head and torso, with these shrimpy legs. He's more or less a Buddha.

When the evaluator left, Henry was exhausted and did his overtired routine that never fails to touch me. He rests on my shoulder silently for a minute, then raises his head, gets really, really close to my face, fixes me with a maniacal stare, then *screams his head off.* As if to say "Can't you see what a crappy world you've brought me into? *I must make you understand.*" He's like a baby as rendered by Edvard Munch.

Still. All in all, it was a day of tender mercies.

April 17, 2002

Orma and I had the Fat Baby conversation again. It goes like this:

Me: Henry's had three bottles and a jar of bananas and it's not 9 A.M. yet.

Orma: Oh. That's OK! I'll just give him some water next time he asks for food.

Me: Great. This is really getting out of hand.

(Ten minutes and some hysterical screaming later)

Orma: He just needs a little more before he takes his nap...

Me: Yes, just a small half-bottle.

Orma: And some peas.

Me: And peas.

(A full bottle and half a jar of peas later: 10 A.M. He's peckish.)

Orma: He likes his food!

Me: Yes, he does!

Orma: Anyone else in your family like their food?

Me: Just me, John, my mother, and everybody else.
(At 10:10 A.M., bellowing)
Orma: It's just a little growth spurt!
Me: Yes, it is! Tomorrow he'll cut down on his own.
Orma: As soon as he starts moving, he'll be trim!
Me: Yes, he will, won't he?

Meanwhile Gus has eaten like one half-bottle and a Tic Tac, and nothing can make him pry his jaws open for solid food.

April 18, 2002
Henry and Gus had their first session with Kim, their personal trainer, which sounds so much better than "physical therapist." Although there was a certain level of complaining (*"You're sitting me up? You're making me reach for that elephant again? No, not the Boppy-Pillow Lean, anything but that"*), by the end they were beaming and gurgling with all the attention paid. Whenever Henry had to do something that tested his capacities, he grunted like a power-lifter: *nnnuuuhhh-UNH*. And the damndest thing is, when I put them on the floor this morning, it was as if they were working out by themselves. Gus, who'd never shown the slightest interest in doing anything other than cooing and kicking while lying on his back, was desperately trying to roll over. Henry was . . . well, actually Henry was just

trying to eat the Gymini, but when I propped him up to sit he actually tried to use his hands to balance instead of doing what he usually does, which is looking at me apologetically as he thuds to the floor.

I imagine both boys would do all this stuff in their own good time, but I keep thinking, well, maybe Kim will keep them from being, like their mother, perpetually picked last for the team.

I DO FIND IT DISCONCERTING, THOUGH, to suddenly have all these people from government agencies coming to my home. What if someone had walked in yesterday at the moment I discovered Henry, who appears not to have a gag reflex, eating one of my shoelaces? It was about three-fourths of the way down his throat before I yanked it out. It occurred to me that if I had to pass a home inspection from an adoption agency, I'd probably fail. The fact that I own another (empty, unused) apartment above this one is not what people coming here see. What they see is two babies and several thousand toys crammed into a living room the size of a hamster cage, blocked off from a steep flight of stairs by a baby gate that keeps breaking. At the foot of the stairs lies an overweight, smelly golden retriever who refuses to move, making trips up and down the stairs with two babies in tow perilous. Nothing besides the electrical outlets is baby-proofed, mostly because if I put all the appropriate locks on toilets and cabinets, *I* won't be able to open them. True, my children are eating regular meals; they're not spearing lizards on the highway median for protein. But there are teetering piles of newspapers and tumbleweeds of dog hair everywhere. In my worst fantasy a government social worker comes to my apartment with one of those handheld UV lights they use on cop shows to illuminate bodily fluids at a crime scene. She switches off the lights, switches on the UV, and my place lights up like a Christmas tree.

April 19, 2002

Any excuse to get out of the house by myself is wonderful. Today's excuse was more wonderful than most. I got to meet someone I hadn't seen in years, an unattainable college crush, one of the brightest, sweetest, funniest guys on campus. Twenty years ago, the joke among his extensive female fan club was that Jim Boylan was the perfect man: certifiably hetero, yes, but with the sweetness, self-deprecating humor, and sensitivity of a woman. Little did we know how right we were.

When Jim, now Jenny, walked in, I thought it was Laura Dern. She's blond, slim, angular, and five foot eleven in tasteful flats; in her long flowered skirt and muted blouse she is dressed like the refined campus hottie she never was.

She'd known from the time she was three that she was a woman, she said; one wife and two children later, she finally had the balls (as it were) to make that internal conviction an outward reality. James Finney Boylan was a college English professor and novelist. Not too surprisingly, Jennifer Finney Boylan just signed a deal for her memoir. We toasted her success with mojitos; while it was a little disconcerting accompanying my former college lust object to the ladies' room, I had to admit she was the same quietly hilarious sweetie I remembered.

It did strike me as ironic, though: here I was, on one of the few child-free days I allowed myself, and while of course I knew about the change, I had vaguely imagined we would be talking about our college, Wesleyan, or his classes, the students, maybe his rock band. Instead, what was I doing? Sitting around with an old girlfriend discussing our kids.

April 20, 2002

When he stays over, which is not very often, John cannot sleep. Somehow this is my fault. We are blessed to have two kids who sleep through the night, yet with John's supersonic hearing, all Gus has to do is make a sound and John's awake for the rest of the night. And when John's awake, he demands company. This is how last night went, after we came home from seeing *Oklahoma* on Broadway. It's 3 A.M.

John: (Sudden cessation of deep breathing sounds. I feel his body go on hyper-alert.)

Gus: Meh.

Me: (Faked heavy-breathing sounds. Don't let John know I'm awake.)

John: Have you thought about the lyrics to "The Farmer and the Cowman"?

Me: (Continued fake heavy breathing, every muscle in body tightening.)

John: It goes, "Oh the farmer and the cowman should be friends, Oh the farmer and the cowman should be friends. One man likes to push a plow, the other likes to chase a cow, but that's no reason why they can't be friends."

Me: (Just keep breathing. Do not engage.)

John: The truth is, there really wasn't that dichotomy. First of all, the farmer didn't push a plow; he had hired help to do it. And the farmer also chased cows, because farmers kept cows. Ranchers also kept some land for crops. So why would the two groups *not* be friends?

Me: Because it's the opening dance number of Act II and Rodgers and Hammerstein were two Jews from Manhattan who didn't know all that much about agriculture. OK? Go back to sleep.

(Silence)

Gus: Meh.

April 29, 2002

I'm pathetically happy. We finally got Gus to eat solid food today—Tender Harvest organic peaches. I had only one jar, which my friend Steven had given me, and I raced all over town trying to find more. Nada. That's because, like a moron, I was looking in obscure health food stores. John found the brand in a Food Emporium and bought the store's entire stock—ten jars.

To celebrate tonight I decided to try the peaches. I have now eaten six of the ten jars. If I can't find more Tender Harvest organic peaches tomorrow, I'm going to kill myself.

May 1, 2002

Dear Playground Police:

I know, on the face of it, it doesn't look good. The baby is small and the dog is large, and the baby's small leg fits very easily in the dog's large mouth. But you'll notice the baby is laughing. Few children giggle when their legs are being gnawed off. Even without your shrieking warnings to alert the rest of the playground populace, rest assured I am on top of the situation.

Kindest regards—

Mother Who Intends to Raise Her Children as Bipeds

May 3, 2002

Just returned from a brunch in a cavernous loft with a woman I barely know and her husband, who's one of the two head writers for *Frasier*. Lovely crowd, but everyone brought their wee germ vectors, who wanted to play with Henry and Gus. For some reason every last one of them were dripping with cold. While hungry would-be TV writers pitched story ideas, ignoring their spawn, who were mashing crepes from Hampton Chutney into the Kashmir rug, John and I found ourselves practically holding Henry and Gus over our heads to keep other kids away. The worst thing about having children? Having to be around other people's children.

I think John is startled by the amount of attention he receives as an old father with two babies. Normally at a party he sits in a corner and glowers. Today he was making the rounds with either Gus or Henry on his arm. They are not just infants. They are props.

May 4, 2002

Had a sex dream last night about the Man in the Yellow Hat. It's something about the way the hat hides his eyes, the way his jodhpurs hug those long, lean thighs. True, he lives with a small annoying monkey and does not seem to seek female companionship. But if you think about it, he's very nurturing. He always comes to George's rescue.

May 5, 2002

"I wrote a note to Gus," Jack tells me. Jack is my seventy-three-year-old dog walker. Though that's not quite accurate. Jack is my seventy-three-year-old polymath and former fashion illustrator who knows more about movies of the thirties and forties than anyone you've ever met; he decided to become a dog walker when his lover of fifty years died and he needed to get out of the house. He and Dale, a Chinese-American artist, were fixtures on New York's downtown arts scene—friends of Andy Warhol who on a typical night might have hung out at the Factory, hopped up on amphetamines and racing through the living room on skates. He also happens to be a twin, whose brother died forty years ago. Jack feels an affinity to Gus, and pangs of foreboding he doesn't discuss with me for Henry. "I told Gus what his life would be like for him," Jack adds.

He and his twin brother, Richard, he tells me, *were* Gus and Henry. Jack was tiny, weak, asthmatic, and covered in eczema. He did poorly in school, being too obstinate to apply himself to anything except what he loved, and spent most of his time in a corner, reading. No one knew he was gay except his brother, though Jack had never actually told him. Richard was Jack's best friend. He was handsome and rugged, an outstanding student, an athlete and immensely successful seducer of women. He was also an alcoholic by the

141

age of fifteen. "Dick seemed invulnerable, but the truth was, everything bothered him," Jack says. "When our father abandoned our mother, he never got over it."

Jack's father, a career man in the navy, was the son of a wealthy Oklahoman family that owned a chain of banks across the Midwest. The last time Jack saw his brother was in a flophouse in California. His wife had left him. His mother had kicked him out of her house. He was covered in sores and shaking. "A doctor? Nah, I don't need anything, Bud," he said. Those were the last words Richard spoke to his brother.

"Everyone thought I was the weak one, but I was steel," Jack tells me. "Look at your sons: Gus is tiny and quiet and slow, but he has inner reserves. Henry is big and strong, but it's Henry who takes everything to heart. Everyone will think he can take anything, and in the end Gus will have to protect him."

It's a lot to forecast for a couple of six-month-olds. But I'm not sure I disagree. I ask Jack to give me the letter; whatever he's said, I'll keep it for Gus and give it to him when he turns eighteen. Jack's eyes narrow and he looks perturbed. "I sort of can't remember where I put it. I was pretty high when I wrote it." I laugh and let the lie stand, but I think, "Someday I'll make sure Gus gets that letter."

May 12, 2002

Happy Mother's Day to me! I bet John will be running out with the boys to get me that Kate Spade coral leather Mia bag I've been ogling. It'll be all wrapped in a beautiful gift box with silver satin ribbon and—oh wait! That probably won't happen because my husband is *halfway across the planet in England with his sister on my first Mother's Day.* I am having to pay Orma to stay here today with the babies so I can pay homage to *my* mother.

While he is gone, though, I am going to live it up. I can leave all the drawers in the kitchen open. My clothing can sit around in random piles, occasionally moving from place to place when the dog decides the piles need to be rearranged. Screw him! I don't have to fill the ice cube trays to the top; I can make midget ice cubes and no one will complain. I am living on the edge.

"It's Mother's Day?" he says, later when we talk. "No, it's not. Mother's Day is—well, I don't know really," he admits. "But not today." First John insists I'm mistaken, then remembers that in England it is celebrated in late March, then gives up on that line of argument when he realizes that *still* means he missed it, then finally apologizes. But he can't let it go. "You used to say this was just a consumerist holiday for selling more flowers and cards. You said holidays like this should be boycotted!"

Do not confuse me with facts. Besides, why does he always take everything I say so literally?

My mother and I had a fine time though. She got to tell me the story of my cesarean birth for the four thousandth time. "Your father gave me six tulips," she says, darting a look of exasperation at Dad, who laughs nervously. "I was so insulted. I expected some jewelry at least."

"What did he do for your first Mother's Day?" I ask.

"*Your* father? *Ha!*" My parents look at each other and smile. They've been married forty-seven years. "That first Mother's Day, I went out with my mother," Mom adds.

May 13, 2002

A horrible day for no reason in particular . . . children whiny and fretful, editors shouting at me because I'm late with stories, money situation dire, nothing getting done. There's a sense of slow, painful yet embarrassing dissolution, like being pecked to death by baby ducks.

Last night I dreamt John had to make love to Jeanne Moreau (that is, the Jeanne of fifty years ago) as part of his conversion process. He was converting to being French. He also had to watch every Godard movie ever made. What infuriated me about the whole thing was his conflating of the two tasks and his complaining about them both. I'm sorry, I know how much you like Jeanne Moreau, stop acting like such a martyr! Having sex with her is not the same as being forced to watch *Alphaville* forty times. Plus, he and Jeanne were very chummy, and when he needed to have sex with her, he was rolling his eyes at me, looking at his watch, and shooing me out of the room. I woke up fuming.

Is there a heart so black as the heart of a woman left alone with her children, when her mate has thought of yet another reason to absent himself? You rage impotently. There is no outlet. You know it's not the fault of the children, any more than it's the fault of maggots for feasting on a corpse. Still, it's all you can do as a rational human being just to throw up your hands and walk out; let the snot-nosed wretches fetch their own bottles and change their own diapers for a few hours.

I think I understand the popularity of *Good Dog, Carl,* and indeed, the entire Carl series. It's not the kids who are enchanted with the idea of a mom leaving the house and the child being cared for by the family rottweiler, it's the *mothers.* We're the ones wistfully poring over the mute pages, watching the baby ride on Carl's back, jump into the laundry basket, have a grand old time, and we're thinking, "*If only . . .*"

The impulse to have children, I think, is the same impulse that drives men to war. There is the promise of emotional extremes that day-to-day life doesn't offer. The thing is, war ends. Motherhood doesn't.

145

May 14, 2002

I slept for nine hours, and they have become cute again. At seven and a half months Henry understands the concept bye-bye but can't seem to master the tidy Queen Elizabeth gesture. Instead he flails both arms up and down so frantically that this morning he clocked himself on the forehead with both hands and ended up bellowing at the top of his lungs.

Gus smiles beatifically as I wave and doesn't move a muscle.

May 16, 2002

Nancy Ney, a photographer I know from the dog run, needs babies to photograph for her portfolio. I explain that neither Henry nor Gus is exactly a Gap child. "That's fine," she said. "Actually, I'm looking for one who's kind of bald and funny-looking." Lady, do I have the baby for you!

The whole thing is kind of a pain, though. We have to go over there with several changes of clothing (no clothing with labels on them—must be generic), and the babies better be well-fed and rested, because they'll be posing with a model. Let's hope the stranger anxiety that's supposed to start any time now doesn't kick in today.

"Repellent, really, the way children are exploited in advertising," I tell myself, as I iron the twelve outfits I bring with me. I have not ironed my own clothes since my last job interview in 1984.

I'M A LITTLE ASHAMED TO SAY we had a great day. You know how people with freakishly large heads often look good on camera? Well, apparently it works for babies too. I always think Gus is angelic-looking, and Henry's well, not. But on camera Henry looks like he was born to sell Pampers, whereas Gus looks like one of those babies you see in a pharmaceutical ad: wan, a little shrunken, peering plaintively out from beneath a headline that reads, *"If it weren't for PediaNex D, this child wouldn't have made it."*

Gus was polite and sweet and long-suffering and smiled, a little; Henry, on the other hand, was practically asking, "Where do I hit my mark?" He burbled and cooed and sucked his toes on cue; he looked meaningfully into the eyes of the male model. And he did this for hours. The only time he cried was when we had to leave. The photographer wants to use him for some real ad, once he can sit up unsupported.

The shame, of course, is twofold: a) giving a shit that my babies performed well for the camera, and b) swelling with pride at having such a rosy, blond (well, what there is of his hair), blue-eyed, vanilla baby. "You want your child to be a commodity?" I mutter to myself in disgust, as I dab concealer over the scratch on his forehead.

May 20, 2002

John's birthday, and it appears everything I do is wrong. No, he does not want to go out. No, he does not want to tell me what he'd like as a present. No and no and no and no. He likes his birthday cake, but does he want to stay over? No. I think it's been several years since we had anything approaching a celebration. And now there is the excuse: the children. It is too expensive or we'll disrupt their bedtime or we have to be back too early, so it's not worth it. In an emergency John's the man to be with. At a party he's the man to avoid. And what use am I to him? I can't cheer him up. I'm not even sure he enjoys my company.

Still, it is wrong to be reading the wedding announcements in the *New York Times* and wishing I could start again. Is there anyone in the world happier than these people? *"The bride and bridegroom worked at Harvard, where she was a research assistant at the child health and social ecology program at the medical school and he was a teaching fellow in the government department. Next month, they will relocate to Goteborg University, where she will begin study for a medical degree and he is to begin a Fulbright fellowship in the university's philosophy department."*

She went to Wellesley and he went to Yale and they're twenty-five and have great hair. They will be married forever and he will be a loving father and he will never turn to her and say, as John said to me last night, "There is no peace or pleasure where there are children."

May 22, 2002
For a story I'm writing on psychics, I went to a famous one today named Carmen. Almost nothing she said even came close to being true. Then she asked me if I had a child—children?—and I mentioned I had twins. She told me what wonderful, creative men they were going to be; how the one born second (Gus) had been my brother in another life, how we'd been together in England, and how he was going to grow up to be a fine pianist. They would grow up to be very good brothers to each other. Oh, and my next book would be fabulously successful. I knew then she was the world's most accurate psychic and I would send everyone I knew to her.

She also said Gus would be the one most affected by John's death. But not to worry, I would never be there to experience all that, since I would die before John. This was a little annoying. What's the point of marrying someone twenty-five years older than you if you don't get to have another husband?

May 23, 2002
They found Chandra Levy's body today, about one year after her disappearance. I remember thinking right before Henry and Gus were born that being Chandra was the worst thing

in the world. Now I think there's something worse: being Chandra Levy's mother.

May 30, 2002

As I left a screaming Henry and Gus with John (I was to be back in two hours, not a minute later, he said, a note of desperation creeping into his voice), I thought, "Reason number 255 women my age are not supposed to have babies." I used to think my jokes that people would think Henry and Gus were my grandchildren were just that— jokes. Then I discovered this: the average age of a first-time grandmother in the United States is forty-seven. So in a sense I owe it to the world (and by "world" I mean "me") to put a fresh face, as it were, on ancient motherhood. Multiple tiny injections with a muscle-paralyzing agent are a small price to pay for looking like I'm not my kids' granny.

A Botox party, for those who don't live in the urban pockets of the U.S. where they are de rigueur, is more or less a Tupperware party for the wrinkly. We socialize, we get a toxin shot into our faces, we leave. When I got there, people were discussing their various self-improvements. "My mantra is: High, tight, and round. High, tight, and round," said my friend Sydney, describing her recent ass-renovation project. I'm here just for the Botox, but after a few glasses of champagne I'm ready to strip down to my underwear and show the doctor, with a laser pointer, the varicose veins I'd like him to remove, the realignment of my breasts to their original upright position, and while he's at it would he mind pulling the skin around my stomach up to my shoulder blades, the way you hoist a cheap pair of pantyhose?

The plastic surgeon finally appeared and began to wax eloquent about our favorite drug. "Not everybody has to inject Botox," he said. "But there are people who don't dye their hair or do their nails either." The gathered women in the room looked at each other quizzically like, *"Have you ever met such a person? Me neither!"*

Eight hundred dollars later, now both drunk *and* paralyzed, I met her. She was the mother of a very famous actress, though she and her daughter were estranged. Mother was clad in dangling earrings and artfully ripped jeans. Her midriff, encircled by a belly chain, peeked out from beneath her shortie lace poet's blouse, the silvery stretch marks visible only to eyes sharper than mine. Her skin was white; her lipstick vermilion. She wore her hair in pigtails—"hair extensions, woven into my real hair like a carpet," she told me. She must have been irresistible when she sported this look—in 1965. Now in her late fifties, she appeared to be emulating her famous daughter. When the plastic surgeon came into the room and she began flirting, coyly pulling at her pigtails, I had to leave.

This woman had her daughter early; she still had the whiff of that youth, a whiff that was rapidly turning into a stench. Well here, at least, is one comfort of having children at forty. One is unlikely to compete with one's teenager. We were old enough to know, when they were born, that the jig was up.

June 4, 2002

I've finally broken down and done the one thing I swore I'd never do: bought videotapes for Henry and Gus. I had to do something. As I was feeding Henry and Gus at 6 A.M. and watching one of my movies on the screen, I noticed their eyes were riveted too. Unfortunately, what I was watching was *Reservoir Dogs.* So rather than doing the unselfish thing— sacrificing my own television at 6 A.M.—I just plunked down a hundred dollars for the complete series of Baby Einstein tapes. These tapes are crack for eight-month-olds. Still, I'm sure they're doing the children a world of good. 'Was that a quotation from Donne or Eliot?" John asks me. "Whose sonata was that?" I ask John. *"Ooh, shiny objects moving fast!"* think Gus and Henry, as their parents continue to inhabit the fantasy world where cheesy hand puppets cavorting to Mozart will get their children into Harvard.

June 20, 2002

Here's something interesting I've learned: when people meet a baby, they desperately want to say something. But let's face it, they don't have a lot to go on. It's not as if they can turn to the baby and say, "Loved your dissertation on the works of J. K. Rowling!" No, with a baby for fodder, you've got the face, and you've got the body. That's it. Everyone's a little scared to say too much about the face. (What if you say how much Timmy looks like Dad, and then you find out Dad was an anonymous sperm donor?) But the body? It's open season. Babyhood is the last time in a person's life where it's socially acceptable to comment on the girth of someone's thighs.

Perhaps I've had more than the usual number of comments from people because a) I have twins, and b) I have twins where one is fat and the other is skinny. Henry was named after my journalistic hero, H. L. Mencken, and kismet being what it is, Henry ended up looking like him as a baby. This is how Mencken described himself: "I was on the fattish side as an infant, with a scow-like beam and noticeable jowls. . . . If cannibalism had not been abolished in Maryland some years before my birth, I'd have butchered beautifully." In a nation where childhood obesity is a huge problem, there's still nothing untoward about having a fat child, as long as that fat child's a boy. The fat girls start getting the weight comments early; Marjorie's daughter Josie, once adorably rotund, was told by strangers to lay off the whole milk. But you see, there's no such thing as a fat boy. He's a bruiser! He's a linebacker! A fat boy can grow up to be James Gandolfini and date supermodels.

But a tiny, skinny boy? I was asked by a stranger if he was getting enough B12 vitamins; I grit my teeth every time I hear the phrase, "Not a lot of meat on his bones, huh?" "Wow, that one's half the size of his brother!" say endless people in astonishment. "You been stealing all your brother's food?" says a man to Henry in Washington Square Park. A guy who works at my supermarket calls them Spaghetti and Meatball. One day I was alone with Henry at the market and he said, "Where's the skinny one?" and without thinking I said, "Oh, his brother ate him." Most unsettling to me was my smirking neighbor, who, every time I'd pass him in the hall, would say, "Well, we can see which one's the favorite, can't we?" That's right, dickwad, there's nothing I enjoy more than starving one kid and shoving food down the other's gullet like a goose being raised for pâté.

I've been dreading Henry and Gus's nine-month checkup. And with good reason. These checkups are like getting a bad report card. And once again, this afternoon I felt like I'd failed. Henry weighs $22^{1}/_{2}$ pounds and is $27^{3}/_{4}$ inches—weight in the 75th percentile, height in the 25th percentile. Short, fat, James Gandolfini. OK. Augustus is 27¼ inches, somewhere between ten and fifteen percent for height. But he weighs 14.3 pounds; he's not even on the charts. There are newborns bigger than he is. I swear to Dr. Deneuve that he's begun to eat, so I'm told I can put off the testing a little while longer.

John's resolve to stay at arm's length from his children weakens whenever I can coax him to come to the doctor's with me. "Poor thing," he mutters over and over as we leave. OK, it's not *that* bad. Gus is just small; he's not an ABC Afterschool Special.

On the way back we stop at a diner, and there discover a fattening food Gus actually seems to love: rice pudding. It's the first time I've seen John smile in weeks. "He will have rice pudding," John intones, as if I'd been purposely hiding the global supply.

When we get home Orma sits on the couch looking glum. She feels like she's failed too.

June 21, 2002

After saying almost nothing in the past twenty-four hours, Orma turns to me and says, "One day I was complaining to my father about something. I don't remember what it was. He say, 'Orma, what's wrong? Don't you believe in God?' That transformed me."

Then she picks up Gus ever so gently, and rubs his feet while he drinks his bottle.

John dashes into the house with a package, opens the refrigerator, rattles around, and dashes out again. I open the refrigerator, and there are three containers of rice pudding stacked neatly on the shelf.

June 25, 2002, Father's Day

I always knew I didn't want a Sensitive New Age Guy as the father of my children—a gusher, a compulsive recorder of Precious Moments, a man who felt he had to be there to cut the cord. (I didn't particularly want to be there, so why should he?) A guy, in short, like the husband of the woman next to me during my stay in the hospital, when I was waiting to deliver Henry and Gus. As his wife lay there, moaning softly, the SNAG alternated between taking long pulls on her bottle of water, trying to talk her into a perineum massage (*"Honey, where did I put the vitamin E oil?"*), and reporting in to his pals on his cell phone: "Yes, we're only dilated six centimeters, but we'll be transitioning soon!" It was all I could do not to shout, "Hey, Pal, *we* are not transitioning, *she* is, and I would like to see *you* try to pass a pot roast through your nostril, which is essentially what she's doing, you skinny little Evian-sucking yuppie doofus."

I also didn't want a man who was more eager to be his children's friend than their father, who believed in negotiating with them and boosting their egos whatever their behavior. (True fact: sociopaths have very high self-esteem!) I thought of this father prototype recently at the playground, while watching a man caring for his toddler son. Every time his two-year-old shoved another child to the ground, Dad would come running over and say, "Now, Harrington, remember that when we hurt others, we hurt ourselves."

God knows I knew I didn't want *that*. But I also didn't count on what I seem to have gotten.

Before we married, John's curmudgeonliness was, to me, the very essence of masculinity. He was inflexible, a man of unerring routine, but also deeply kind and generous. I always knew he would do anything for me; I also knew he would grouse incessantly while doing it. The ability to be charming and glib were overrated qualities, I thought; a man who broods is a man who is really present in this world. He loves silence and rainstorms and intelligent debate; he hates parties and gossip and sunny days. He was a classicist in his tastes, from music to furniture, nostalgic about the past and deeply cynical about the future. John is not someone who would take lemons and make lemonade. He is someone who would take lemons and explain to you for five hours how lemons used to have a finer balance of sweetness to sourness, but now, with modern agricultural techniques, they were made to look fresh and appealing but were in fact far inferior in taste. And he would be right. Annoying, but right.

Unfortunately, the bulldog qualities that made him so appealing (and sort of amusing) as a husband aren't working so well as a father. Having children necessitates the ability to look sunnily to the future—to overlook the tantrums and the cacophony of dementedly chattering toys and the smells and the tears and the orange slices sucked dry, then hurled to the floor. Children are a mess. John is not.

Today, John's first Father's Day, I have many wishes. I wish John would change a diaper or give a bath. I wish he'd stop calling the babies "disease vectors." I wish he would stop reminding me of how much private school costs every time I look longingly at a new pair of Manolos. Henry is, um, an unusual-looking baby. But I wish he could let it go already. "Hey, look, Henry got a part in this movie!" John whispers to me, as we watch Gollum frolic in *Lord of the Rings: The Two Towers*.

And I wish I could stop thinking of Amy, his love for so many years. It's not that I live, *Rebecca*-like, in her shadow; it's that Gus and Henry do. Amy had no family other than John; John cared for her tenderly, through so many illnesses, for twenty years. It's not his lack of responsibility, but an overdeveloped sense of it, that makes John dread fatherhood so. When he complains about the two small lives he's been entrusted with, I try to remember where he's been and where he thought he'd never have to go again. It's not that he doesn't care; it's that he cares too much to feel a sense of joy.

I know all this. I do. I still adore him. There's also a good percentage of the time I imagine him hanging from a meat hook. If we're going to stay together, I wish someone would tell me how.

June 27, 2002

Beware the skinny food critic, I thought last night, as I marveled for the hundredth time how my dear college friend Sam, whose sensuality did not extend to his palate, had become one of New York's top restaurant reviewers. John and I were ungrateful wretches, really, supping at his table and mocking him—his reverence for the uncannily precious, the one-ingredient-too-many dishes, and his rejection of the lush and obviously delicious. "Did you ever stop to consider that 'warm chocolate melting cake' is a restaurant cliché because it's actually *good* and people want to eat it, as compared to most of the stuff you like?" I say. Sam smiles and ignores me, scribbling on his notepad yet another vile dish that New Yorkers will scramble to order after his review comes out on Wednesday. I love Sam. I hate his taste in food. It was around midnight by the time we left, John heading uptown and I downtown, to our respective apartments.

The succession of thoughts that went through my mind after being punched in the stomach by a random crazy person while I walked through Grand Central were a) hmm, I hope she didn't surreptitiously stick me with a needle, and b) this will teach me to leave my kids home with the sitter till midnight. Three hundred pounds of hulking womanhood punching me, leaving me doubled over and gasping, for no reason, then lumbering away at an extremely slow clip. Yet she got away. By the time we could find police, she'd slipped into the crowd.

In truth I was glad John wasn't there, because he would have done something butch and tomorrow we'd be in the middle of a lawsuit. But John couldn't forgive himself. "I'm deflated," he said. He was awake all night, thinking he had failed me. I plan to milk his guilt to slip out to a movie this weekend.

Is this why parents become cautious stay-at-homes? Living, in the sense of breathing and functioning, becomes way more important than having a life. A baby's message to a parent is, "Just be there! We don't care if you can't carry on a conversation about the latest movie or opening of a restaurant; in fact, we'd really prefer you didn't, because every time you step away from us there's a chance you won't be back."

The whole incident also made me question the wisdom of living in separate apartments now that we have children. Maybe we are frisky, unconventional people who don't see any need to be suffocated by the constant presence of another. On the other hand, maybe there's something wrong with us. Years ago when I read Gide's *The Vatican Cellars,* one passage about a husband and wife stuck in my mind:

> *They had no sooner settled in Rome than they arranged their private lives independently of each other—he on his side, she on hers; Veronica in the care of the household and in the pursuit of her devotions, Anthime in his scientific researches. In this way they lived beside each other, close to each other, and just able to bear the contact by turning their backs to one another. Thanks to this they regained a kind of harmony between them; a sort of semi-felicity settled down upon them; the virtue of each found its modest exercise in putting up with the faults of the other.*

Forget the death and mayhem to follow; at the time I read that, I thought, "Wow, now that's the way to live! Touching, but not so much as to bruise." Today I read that passage and see what Gide saw: that sometimes distant politeness is a silent scream. John faithfully comes over to the house every evening and leaves most nights. Were John and I Anthime

and Veronica, living closely, with our backs turned? No
wonder Anthime thrusts a flaming-hot penknife in his thigh.

June 28, 2002

As if I didn't dread the weekends without Orma enough,
Henry whined from the moment he woke up to the moment
he went to bed. It was such an awful day that at one point in
Toys "R" Us, I was looking wistfully at every toy that said
"Small parts: Choking hazard." As we were heading back
home and stopped for a latte at Barnes & Noble, John
picked the also-whimpering Gus out of his carriage and
promptly found himself plastered in shit. Lucky it was Gus,
not Henry. Henry is in a hundred little ways like his father:
loud, complaining, strong, nosy, restless, affectionate, male.
He gets on John's nerves. Gus—tiny, delicate, quiet,
musical, cherubic, a little distant—is his pet. "Poor thing,"
John murmurs to his soiled child. "Poor thing." It's easy for
John to forget Gus is a boy.

June 29, 2002

At Marjorie's urging, I finally took Augustus to a Music
Together class in the basement of a local church in the
East Village. Augustus, the baby who vibrates with
pleasure whenever I play anything by Mozart, will love
this class, I think.

Kelly, the East Village hipster girl teaching the class, had biceps like Linda Hamilton in the second *Terminator.* She looked beautiful, if a little strung out. She began to sing: *"Hello, everybody, it's so nice to see you! Hello, Gus, it's nice to see you! Hello, moms and dads, it's so nice to see you! Hello, nannies, it's so nice to see you! Hello, ceiling, it's so nice to see you! Hello, mirror, it's so nice to see you!"*

How long did it take, sixty seconds? thirty? before I realized that if I had to spend forty-five minutes in Music Together, I would be climbing the water tower. Alexis, Josie, and Maisy were with their mothers; India, Lucas, Ruben, and Dashiell were with their nannies; Zachary was toted by his father. Dad had an extremely expensive, tiny digital movie camera trained on Zachary every second; he did not want to miss that magic moment when his son learned to shake bells in time to the music. So preoccupied was Dad with capturing Zachary's close-up that it took him about a minute to notice his son was deep-throating the handle of a castanet and was quite close to impaling himself.

Gus took in the situation quickly and somewhere between the crumb-chasing mouse song and "Two Little Kitty Kats" he proceeded to become autistic, choosing to visit a pleasant land far, far away. He refused to look at me, the other babies, or the scarf I was frantically waving over his head, in time to the beat of "Obwesanasa."

The music made Barney seem like Marilyn Manson but even so, by the end of the class many of the babies were either sobbing piteously or, if they were mobile, scurrying for the door. "There's been a lot of research on this," says Kelly, "and children who come from cultures where folk songs are sung to them all the time in the same scale have a higher incidence of people with perfect pitch." The parents nodded their heads, looking hopeful. Kelly then proceeded to sing "Good-bye, farewell, we'll see you all again" at a pitch best heard by dogs.

Maybe it was just a problem with Kelly; maybe we'll try again in a few months. Right now we're sticking with Mozart and show tunes.

July 10, 2002

Exasperated. Augustus saw Maureen the developmental specialist today. I made sure she came right after his nap, so he was well rested and alert and able to perform his little tricks and stunts. But the things he does all the time normally, he very sweetly refuses to do in front of her. You drop a washcloth on his head, which he normally whips off: he leaves it there. You give him a little toy, which he passes from hand to hand, and which he can drop and then retrieve without looking at it. In front of Maureen, he looks at it like, *"What's that? A toy, you say? I say it's dangerous, and I am going to stare it down with my laser vision until it vaporizes."* Most alarmingly, at ten months he doesn't answer to his own name.

Finally she leaves, tactfully telling me the "homework" I have to do with Augustus. At this point, after also being worked out by Kim the physical therapist, he is crying. So Maureen and Kim go down my stairs, waving bye-bye, and the second they are out of sight he starts laughing. I know it is just a chortle, but to me it sounds like *mwah-hahahahaha.*

Kim comes back for a second to ask me something and sees him laughing, and he gets this look on his face like, "Oops." She starts to laugh and I say, "Wait, just hide for a second." She hides, I wait for a bit, talking to someone else; then stop and say, "Augustus?" and he immediately turns toward me with his curious "You rang?" expression.

What gets to me is that he's so sweet in his subversiveness. He doesn't do anything which would give these evaluators a sense he's in a bad mood—doesn't cry or whine or express distress in any way. At least if he did that, they might think they'd caught him at a bad time. Instead, he smiles dreamily and refuses to do anything, as if to say, "Hi, I'm completely retarded! Isn't it sad? But don't feel bad for me, because I'm oblivious to the fact that my future career is bussing tables at Denny's."

July 15, 2002

Augustus found his penis today. When he made the discovery he got real quiet. I think it was a sacred moment for him. I'm imagining years of girls having to endure tiresome Tantric sex lectures.

July 20, 2002

Orma is melancholy. She is thinking of James, the little boy she took care of for four years. She would love to call, to see how he is doing. "He is a bright little boy—brilliant!" she says. (Of course, Orma has never cared for a child she didn't think was brilliant.) From the time he was five weeks old she cared for him. She loved that little boy. She loved his sister too. Sophia. "I think you know when some children approve of you, you say, Oh my God, I'm really a good person."

At first Sophia didn't like having a new nanny for her baby brother, but over time she too came to love Orma. At night she would crawl into Orma's bed. And that's when Orma's problems began. Sophia followed Orma around like a pup. James started calling her "Mommy." When the mother of the lady of the house came to stay, she convinced her daughter that little James's love of Orma was "unhealthy," and if he were ever to have a proper relationship with his mother, Orma had to go. So instead of thanking God every day of her life that her kid had more than one person he loved and trusted, she sent Orma packing. And to this day, Orma pines.

"America is a different culture from Jamaica, you know," she says. "In Jamaica, if you live with children and treat them well, they appreciate you. In America, you treat the children well, they love you, the parents are upset. They get rid of you. They don't care."

Henry and Gus pretty much know who's who, but every now and then they call Orma "Mama." Now I understand why she shakes with embarrassment when they do this. "No, *that* is Mama! *That* is Mama!" she yells, and she'll drag them over to me and point and practically jump up and down. I've told her I don't care, that they'll figure out who Mom is before high school. I am just so grateful they greet her with shining eyes every time she walks through the door.

July 21, 2002

I do wish things would stop disappearing from the house, though.

No, it's not that. No one is more honest. It's just that Orma doesn't like my taste. I can't say I blame her.

It started innocently enough, with food. If she saw anything in the refrigerator she believed had been there too long, she would throw it out. Unfortunately her sense of when something spoiled was heavily influenced by growing up in a hot climate without a refrigerator; I think she was convinced any foodstuff that had lain around more than twelve hours would poison Henry and Gus. Why take chances? And why ask the mother? She once caught me making formula from water that was not, strictly speaking, boiled. At that moment I believe I lost all credibility.

Then there was the day I realized I had a new bathroom rug. I had no memory of buying one. I did remember Orma had remarked on how much she disliked the color of the old one. So once the color of the rug had changed from blue to heather green, other elements in the bathroom had to change too. One day I had a new toothbrush holder, and a week later, there were towels. It is true that my old towels had holes. She doesn't like to argue with me about these things. She just makes the old items quietly disappear. Then they are replaced with other things, and I am presented with the bill. Growing up in poverty, she can't understand why someone who seems, in her mind, wealthy would have towels with holes. She doesn't say this, of course. To me she says only, "I like beauty."

I know I have to do something about this but I just can't bring myself to discuss it. Today, moody and nostalgic, she was looking at my shower curtain with a gimlet eye.

July 22, 2002

Just came back from the photo shoot for the shots that will accompany my new parenting column. John stared at me blankly for a moment, then announced, "You look dreadful." Getting my curly hair blown stick-straight: not one of my better ideas. But the hair guy was all, "Oh, this is fabulous on you!" He was also suggesting we could tie my hair in a big pink scrunchie and have Fun! so perhaps I shouldn't have listened.

But at least I had the pleasure of seeing Henry and Gus be the very best babies it's possible to be. It was oppressively hot and sticky in the studio; they were kept waiting for over an hour; and the most Henry did to express his displeasure was spit up a little on the white photo paper. Both were so sweet and cooperative, despite no naps and a gaggle of strangers hovering over them with lights and shadow-blockers and enormous-lensed cameras. I was practically crying after an hour, but they were fine.

When a stylist and fashion director confer quietly about you and the words you keep hearing are "We can Photoshop that," you know it's not your finest hour.

July 23, 2002

At yesterday's shoot, one of the stylists asked me the question I've probably been asked more often than any other since Henry and Gus were born: *"So, are you in love?"*

When they were newborns I think I offended everyone by being honest. Love them? Not by any definition of love I had at forty. I could only love someone I knew, and I didn't know them. What people call "love" with babies is the tenderness that comes from pity, combined with the urgency of being needed like you've never been needed before. We love the touch of a baby's skin, of course, and those fragrant hot heads. But it took many months for them to become particular—not generic babies, but my babies.

During those first few months, as I went through those simple yet relentless everyday tasks that add up to motherhood, I learned something interesting. I'd made a huge mistake. Not a mistake in becoming a mother—I was still on the fence about that one—but a mistake in thinking I had to go through those years of infertility treatment because I needed a child that was tethered to me biologically. I feared without the DNA connection, I might never have felt the love. I couldn't have been more wrong. The real love comes not from DNA but from the wrestling on of the onesie, the relief of the burp at 2 A.M., the nail clipping and the nose suctioning and the glorious silence of satisfaction when the warm bottle reaches trembling lips. Curiously, love comes from fussing, not from gestating. But nobody could have convinced me of that as I was shooting another vial of Fertinex into my ass at six in the morning.

July 24, 2002

Another seething, silent feud with Orma. Seemingly overnight Augustus has gone from eating nothing to devouring anything handed to him, and in my overzealousness to see him eat I occasionally give him food he gags on. "Why you do that?" she demands, as Gus coughs up a cookie. *"Because I'm trying to asphyxiate my son,"* I want to scream, *"and by the way, where are my penguin mugs?"*

Several mugs that had penguins in a lovely abstract pattern—admittedly, a pattern that on closer inspection revealed them to be humping—have vanished. Apparently Orma has made enough headway in the bathroom, and now she's working on the kitchen.

July 25, 2002

Today's jolt of happiness: the steady *smack-smack-smack* of Henry's hands against the parquet floor as he crawled towards me, grim and tortoiselike, a furrow on his brow and his jaw set in determination to reach my desk and gnaw on the computer wires.

But it's been a trying day. I decided this morning that, rather than paying eighty-nine cents for a jar of what amounts to half a banana, I will make the colossal effort of mashing a fresh banana myself. Whoo! So I mash away and give it to Henry, who makes a variety of bewildered faces. Banana project completed, I turn around to put the dish in the sink, and when I come back he is a photo ripped from a medical textbook, huge red blotches everywhere, eyes swollen, neck crimson, eyes bugging out. WTF? Of course at that moment Orma walks in. She goes over to pick up Henry, who's now crying, then stares accusingly at me. "He eats jars of bananas all the time!" I exclaim as I dial the pediatrician.

I knew enough to realize that if his breathing's OK, he doesn't have to be rushed immediately to the ER. But I didn't know whether something would happen to his breathing soon. I get the pediatrician's nurse on the phone; she tells me just to watch him but to keep some liquid Benadryl on hand just in case. I run to the drugstore, and by the time I return in ten minutes it is as if nothing happened; he is his usual peaches-and-cream self. My theory is that the sheer novelty of my delicious homemade treat threw him into an ecstasy, and lacking the ability to verbalize his joy, he somatized his emotions and broke out in hives. Either that, or he's allergic to uncooked bananas.

"Why you give him banana?" Orma asks, for the fifth time

today. The way she asks the question, it is clear she believes I am aware of my children's allergies but am performing secret science experiments on them, all part of my plan for world domination.

July 26, 2002

Today Gus was diagnosed with sensory integration issues, which as far as I can tell means he doesn't remove a sock puppet from his foot fast enough. I think Gus's thought process goes something like this: "Dididididi, oh look, there's a dragon on my foot...dididididi... look at those big eyes...dididididi...Hey, fur!...dum dum dum dum...OK, time for sock to come off." He studies it, whereas apparently the normal reaction is supposed to be "Puppet—off."

Maybe I'm oversimplifying. At ten months he doesn't put a lot of stuff in his mouth (no exploring), has aversions to unfamiliar tastes and textures, looks kind of scared when a stranger whirls him in the air, and so on.

"There are people who go through their whole life unable to stand loud noises, or finding massage unpleasant, or being driven nuts by the sensation their hands are dirty," said Irene, the occupational therapist evaluating Gus. John and I glanced at each other; I wondered if she'd noticed how many times I had washed my hands since she arrived. John cannot abide most noise; a truck idling outside our window is enough to keep him up for hours. As a child I would scream if someone tried to put me in a sandbox; I can't put moisturizer on with my bare hands because I can't stand the feeling of anything slimy. Certainly I can't even imagine having a massage. Why would you want a stranger to touch you if he wasn't having sex with you? It doesn't compute.

And yet both John and I managed to make it to adulthood. It's interesting how what was once considered a quirk is now considered a pathology. A pathology desperately in need of medical intervention. Still, if someone is willing to come to my house and make my son stop crying when he touches Play-Doh, I'm all for it.

August 1, 2002

I worry that Marjorie thinks I love her for her pool. She's right, of course, but can you blame me? How many other people in the East Village have a backyard, let alone a genuine, in-the-ground swimming pool in their backyard? On this sweltering day Marjorie, her husband, Jonathan, and their daughter, Josie, who is Henry and Gus's age, hosted a pool party for a dozen babies and their parents. While Josie and her little friends shrieked with joy in the water, Henry and Gus clung to me like baby baboons when I tried to commit the act of swimming. They were all, "What is this bottomless abyss of wet? It is cold; there are no bubbles; we are being sent here because *we've done something very, very wrong.*"

My friend Jackie had come with me. She was the first among my friends from college to have a child, and the first to have a child whose company I loved. She and her husband separated when Jack was born. Jack was funny, smart, and loving; impossible sometimes, too, but brimming with curiosity and enthusiasm. How do you raise an eleven-year-old boy in New York City who has not a nasty or sarcastic word to say about anyone? It always seemed a miracle to me. So Jackie is my role model for motherhood; I pay attention to what she does the way the average ten-year-old pays attention to Britney Spears.

Today Jackie was hanging out, drinking margaritas out of huge plastic Prozac cups (Marjorie's father is a psychiatrist) and making sure Henry and Gus didn't drown. I saw a mother approaching her with that familiar covetous look in her eye and I tried to head her off. But it was too late. "How long have you been working for Judith?" asked the woman. Jackie is tall, beautiful, regal, and black. "Uh, about five minutes?" she said. Jackie and I can't go to any gathering of mothers where someone doesn't ask the question. I am mortified. Jackie is not. "Hey, they want to *steal* me from you," she says gleefully.

Mothers milled about, watching other people's children the way farmers eye livestock at a 4-H show. One mother, an East Village momzilla named Katrina in a Tibetan embroidered smock and a long gray braid down her back, asked me casually what words Henry and Gus were saying. Then she asked me again. And again. I think she wanted me to draw up a list. I was about ten seconds from saying, "Don't worry, they're mutes. They may never speak! If it makes you feel any better, I think they're blind too."

"Of course," she said, her voice dropping conspiratorially, "we can't compare our sons to Josie. Josie is a prodigy. She's a *freak.*"

"Not too many people know this, but Marjorie's a ventriloquist," I continued, chewing the ice from my fourth margarita. "Go ahead, try to get Josie talking when Marjorie's not around." Katrina was silent for a moment, filing away this information for further processing and assessment later.

"I see your Gus has a pacifier," she continued. "Harrison has never needed one, thank God. Do you know how long you're going to allow it?"

"It's something that keeps me up at night," I said, "because I know how heartbreaking it will be when he's refused admission to colleges because he can't go to an interview without his *binkie.*" Katrina's lips tightened, and she walked away. I think Marjorie's going to stop inviting me to her parties.

All in all a lovely day, if bittersweet. So interesting to be around all those fathers who were genuinely enjoying their children.

John didn't come with me. He hates the sun.

August 3, 2002

We should probably stop calling Henry "Fat Man," since that is now the name he answers to. Unfortunately, he is more deserving of the title than ever. John and I have taken to saying comforting things to each other like, "Well, at least his giant head balances out his enormous bulk!" Henry's life goal right now is to destroy my apartment. I left him alone for sixty seconds, and when I returned he had managed not only to tear off the glass door of the cabinet that holds my VCR but also to dismantle the cabinet's entire wooden frame. I still don't know how he did this. Hell, I don't think *I* could have done it. A few days ago we were visiting a friend and her husband, and I see Henry dragging something round in a leather case from room to room. "Hey, that's my bowling ball," my friend's husband said. I think of Henry as Bam-Bam. I may rent him out to people who are baby-proofing their homes. In fifteen minutes, they can learn exactly what items in their homes can be pulled off shelves, opened, ripped off hinges, shredded, spilled, gnawed on, and catapulted across the room by twenty-four pounds of pure evil.

Gus, thankfully, has mastered sitting, just shy of his eleven-month birthday. He is remarkably resourceful at keeping his toys from being pinched by Henry, whose other pleasure in life is to grab whatever Gus is playing with. Since Gus has no strength, he has to use his wiles; it's remarkable to see how he maneuvers objects from one side to another, clutching them with his feet as well as his hands, to keep them away from his brother.

I think I need to get Henry a helmet. He's hoisting himself upright on the furniture, holding on for a bit, and then in a triumphant, Rocky-like gesture thrusting both fists into the air, thus catapulting himself backwards onto his head. And every time he does it, he is surprised.

August 16, 2002

Yesterday I went to a hand surgeon to find out why I've been in pain for months. I figured it was probably a ganglion cyst and I'd need to have it removed. Either that or it was some sort of repetitive stress injury. The surgeon moved my hand back and forth. "Do you have a baby?" he asked. As it turns out, there's a particular kind of tendonitis (DeQuervain's) that

women get from babies—something about the way we hook
our thumbs under their arms when we lift them. Who knew?

This week it's the tendonitis. Last week it was my back.
Forty-one-year-olds are supposed to be hosting soigné dinner
parties, reading serious literature, or perhaps basking on the
beach at St. Bart's, enjoying a well-earned vacation from a
stressful yet interesting career. They are not supposed to be in
the playground, crawling through a wee tunnel like a prairie
dog, trailing an eleven-month-old bent on self-annihilation.
Until last week I would have said my favorite drug was
Botox. Now I can say it's Percodan, and plenty of it.

What with the fatigue and the back and tendonitis, I was
up last night worrying about our ages. Will I be around
when Gus first headlines at Carnegie Hall (or Vegas, I'm not
picky)? Will I be there for Henry's first, second, and third
marriages? Other kids are going to be skiing and playing
tennis with their parents at thirty, and Henry and Gus are
going to be wheeling us around with our oxygen tanks.
(Well, they'll be wheeling me. Dad should be so lucky.)

I find myself with more than a passing interest in
nematodes. Researchers at the University of California, San
Francisco have found that by creating certain genetic
alterations in a nematode, a tiny worm, they can not merely
double their lifespan but keep them *frisky*. When the UCSF
brainiacs decide it's time to experiment on something a

little more complex than a nematode, I'll be the first to volunteer.

August 24, 2002

A baby's entire life comes down to testing this proposition: "I wonder what will happen if I do *this*"—"this" being something that will kill said baby. But baby doesn't know! Still tries! Then gets hit on the head and loses a few more IQ points. It's so cute.

But knowing this as I do didn't prevent me from being a very bad mother today. After Henry pulled Gus's hair for the tenth time (all the while looking over at me to see what I'd do), and after I unclenched his tiny fist for the tenth time and after Gus howled for the tenth time (I was counting), I finally gave Henry a slap on the hand. A tiny one—more like a flick, really—but his eyes got big and his lower lip started to tremble and then he flat-out bawled, more with the indignity of the slap than anything else, I think.

I felt like sewage. I was still berating myself when Monty came over to me at dinner, seemingly looking for affection, and as I was petting him he grabbed the remainder of my hamburger off my plate. He's never done this before. If I can't get Monty to respect me—a *golden retriever,* for Christ's sake, the easiest breed of dog to train in the universe—what chance do I have with my children?

Henry has stopped pulling Gus's hair, though. Of course, now he's probably planning to shoot him in the neck with a poison blow dart.

September 1, 2002

Dare I hope the children are becoming a little more interesting to John? He still lies in bed and says things like, "I remember us before babies and dogs, when there was some pleasure in life." Still, Henry and Gus are pretty much the only conversation he has with his friends. He talks about them like they're some sort of ongoing engineering project. Coming out of his mouth it always sounds like he, John, has personally designed Henry's legs and has tinkered with Gus's appetite so that they are now in fine working order.

I just wish for John's sake I could tone down Henry's shrieking. All it takes is my walking into the room, Orma's arrival in the morning, a plate of peaches, and it's *eeeeeeeeeeeeeeeeeeeeeeeeeeeeeeeeeeeeeeeee!* It's like living with a pterodactyl. I try to remind myself it's an expression of youthful exuberance, and wouldn't it be great if *we* felt that excited about a plate of peaches? But I'm forty-one; I've spent the last few years assiduously avoiding youthful exuberance.

September 3, 2002

"C'mon, it'll be fun!" How often have I heard these words from Jackie over the years? And how often have they landed us in emergency rooms? The last time Jackie convinced me to go away with her and her son, Jack was to a house in upstate New York without air-conditioning during what turned out to be the hottest weekend in New York in the last decade. The ER visit came when Jack, sweltering and covered in mysterious welts, required oxygen and steroids for his asthma at three in the morning. The welts quickly subsided, and we thought no more about them until we returned to New York a few days later. At that point Jackie called and mentioned in passing, "Jack has chicken pox. I assume you've had them already, right?" So in actuality that vacation entailed two visits to the hospital: one then, and one when the pox covering every inch and orifice of my body led to pneumonia. When John wants to disgust me, he trots out the photos from those weeks.

So at any rate, when Jackie utters the words "C'mon, it'll be fun!" you'd think I'd flee so quickly all that would be left would be a cartoon puff of smoke. But Jackie can be persuasive, and if, like her, you were born with a congenital inability to predict the consequences of your actions, the idea of taking two eleven-month-olds and a golden retriever to an ancient, non-baby-proofed bed-and-breakfast near the ocean sounds like a rollicking good time.

I admit, maybe I didn't ask the right questions. But when the owner of a bed-and-breakfast exclaims "We love babies!" and "My niece has triplets!" I can be excused for thinking they were prepared, in some modest fashion, for the arrival of actual flesh-and-blood infants. A couple of cribs, some high chairs, maybe a room with a tub? But no. There's nothing an eleven-month-old likes better than sitting on a cement floor of a shower while a tsunami cascades down on the unfused bones of his head.

We arrived in the evening and almost immediately shut ourselves in my chintz-infested room so as not to disturb our fellow travelers, who seemed more disturbed than necessary to see two babies at a B&B. There were whispers, rolled eyes. I hated children who didn't belong to me too, but this was a little excessive, I felt.

Amid the riot of wicker and cross-stitching there was no place for Henry and Gus to sleep but the floor or my bed. They'd never slept in bed with me before, or with each other. "This is fun!" they seemed to say. So fun that they never stopped moving, and despite my frantically clutching them to my chest like Daffy Duck with his pearls (*"mine, mine, all mine"*), they both managed to fall off the bed with a gigantic thud. Then they cried piteously for bottles, necessitating firing up the microwave three flights down from my room.

At 6:30 A.M. we stumbled downstairs, where Jackie and I did what we could to stop the children from wilding. Then a climb back up the rickety staircase. "This is where we serve breakfast!" chirped the proprietor, ushering us to a rooftop terrace unmarred by a guardrail or even a rail: that would have blocked the lovely view of the ocean, but perhaps prevented my children from fulfilling the wish now uppermost in their hearts, namely to crawl off the roof into the shrubbery forty feet below. We ate Cheerios dampened with formula in my room.

The fine mist of rain that greeted our arrival had not let up, but we dutifully pushed Henry and Gus in their stroller and deposited them gently on the beach. It was chilly and a little damp. On cue they held their arms above their heads and howled. If they could have managed it, they would have been balancing themselves on tiptoe on an individual grain of sand.

"Isn't this great?" said eleven-year-old Jack. Jackie and I looked at each other. "They may not be beach guys yet," Jack continued, ignoring Henry's screeches as he trickled sand on his knee, "but just give them a chance!" The dog, who'd been swimming, took that opportunity to waddle up to Henry and Gus and shake off the freezing water, then turned around to dig a hole, kicking the sand onto Gus. Gus collapsed in existential despair.

I had known Ocean Grove was a Methodist community before I came, though I had not known that there was literally a fence around the perimeter so that cars could not drive in on the Sabbath or that liquor was not served in the town. No town that does not serve liquor can possibly be called "baby-friendly."

In an hour the mist had turned into a downpour, and between that, the accommodations, and the rules about drinking, a second night here seemed about as desirable as being Winona Ryder's personal shopper. Still, Jackie was convincing me that we should give it another night— *"C'mon, it'll be fun!"*—when I finally found out why we'd been the source of so much nudging and pointed stares. There was another group staying at the B&B, a group of like-minded individuals who had a Listserv on the Internet and who were meeting here for the first time—a local chapter of Childless by Choice. *"Oh, we love babies!"* *Fuck you, ye olde dimwits.*

On our way back to the city, sheets of rain pounded the Jeep and the children screamed. At the best of times I'm a nervous driver and now, with hydroplaning in my immediate future, I was one raw nerve. I clutched the wheel, my knuckles icy and white. In the seconds before lightning the air was thick with the smell of peat; then the relucent sky, the blast of thunder, and Gus screaming so violently he threw up. Seizing this delightful and unexpected snacking opportunity, the dog materialized from the Jeep's back seat to lick Gus clean.

Jack momentarily glanced up from the book he was reading. "Only twenty more years to go!" he said.

September 5, 2002

> *Me:* Henry and Gus are going to need a haircut soon.
>
> *Orma:* No.
>
> *Me:* No?
>
> *Orma:* Not yet. They need some words.
>
> *Me:* ?
>
> *Orma:* They must say "Mama" and "Papa." If you cut their hair before they can say your name, you take away their strength.

September 6, 2002

Orma asked me about Henry and Gus's one-year birthday party. When were we starting the preparations? Naturally I laughed it off. What preparations? With the renovation on the apartment upstairs not even begun, there was no room downstairs and just a large empty raw space upstairs; did she think I was going to hold a party up there? Or did she think I was going to *rent a space* for a bunch of one-year-olds, who hadn't the slightest clue what they were celebrating?

As I explained all this, Orma looked at me and nodded. Then she walked away.

September 10, 2002

Orma has been unusually quiet lately. Today is my cousin Laurie's birthday, and when I was leaving to meet my family at the restaurant she said to wish Laurie a very happy birthday. I tried to tell her that we weren't, for the most part, a family that was big on celebrations, but by this time she was upstairs reading a story to the boys.

September 15, 2002

As soon as the boys have some idea what a party is, I explain, we will have a big one. When they're three—tons of kids! Games! Prizes! Clowns! (OK, not clowns. Never clowns.) Orma nods and gives Gus his rice pudding.

September 16, 2002

"You know what's most hateful about kids' parties?" I say to Orma, not that the topic has come up. "The frenetic competition in Manhattan to have the biggest, the best. A plastic surgeon I knew had her one-year-old's party catered by Glorious Foods. There was a band, strolling cowboys, a petting zoo. Ponies! How many one-year-olds can ride a pony? I resent that my big nose and the bags under my eyes paid for her little exercise in decadence."

At this point I'm shouting. Orma's eyes are cool and appraising.

September 18, 2002
Orma is on the phone with her sister Yvonne. When I come into the room, she hangs up.

September 20, 2002
You only turn one once.

September 25, 2002
It took most of the morning to blow up the balloons and make tiny gift bags filled with party favors. As I work the nozzle to the helium tank I hear Sylvia Plath:

> Your small
> Brother is making
> His balloon squeak like a cat.
> Seeming to see
> A funny pink world he might eat on the other side of it,
> He bites,
> Then sits

Back, fat jug
Contemplating a world clear as water
A red
Shred in his little fist.

I was afraid to ask Orma how many nannies and children
were coming, but there seemed to be enough curried
chicken, plantains, and rice and peas to open a Jamaican
restaurant. The bill for cupcakes alone came to over $100—
$3.50 apiece—but they are so lovely, with the buttercream
violets on top. Too bad Henry and Gus don't eat cupcakes.

With Elvis singing gospel in the background, a dozen
babies I'd never seen before and their nannies piled into my
empty upstairs apartment. We even had a celebrity baby—
Natasha, Norman Mailer's granddaughter. Orma wanted to
hold the party at the Central Park Zoo. I congratulated
myself for standing firm.

Frankly, I don't remember much of what happened next,
because I started drinking and everything became more
pleasant. The booze dulled the pain of Thea. Thea is a
beautiful little blond girl who, at the age of one, has the
vocabulary of an Oxford don. While Henry and Gus are still
wrapping their minds around "baba" and "dada," Thea was
diligently handing objects to my father—duckie, elephant,
CD—and labeling them. "Henry and Gus can't do that!"

said my father, helpfully. Thea then asked her nanny if we had broccoli for lunch. She is a devil baby. She left the party in a trail of sulfur fumes, and I just know right this minute she's handing toys to Satan and saying "duckie" in her perfect, fluting English.

No one-year-old party is complete without bloodshed, and little Graham provided it when one of the nannies stepped on his fingers, somehow tearing a nail from its bed. Graham's nanny, who had apparently been sequestered in the bathroom doubled over with cramps, came out, found Graham white with pain and hysterical, and then *she* started to cry. Orma and the other nannies passed the screaming, bloody child around while his nanny wrung her hands and I called his parents. I knew Graham would be fine, but I did have a moment of panic when I discovered both his parents were lawyers.

Henry and Gus, dressed by Orma in plaid shirts and jeans and looking like wee lumberjacks, became increasingly terrified by the cacophony and ended the afternoon clutching their bottles and heaving small, heartrending sobs. They did get a nice haul of presents, though, and my parents seemed to have a good time.

John hid downstairs in our bedroom.

Orma was very happy.

September 26, 2002

All parents wonder what their child will be like when he grows up. At the dawn of their second year, am I wrong in imagining Henry and Augustus will be very much who they are now?

Henry is blond and blue-eyed and fair, with a startling deep *heh-heh-heh* chortle that makes people turn around on the streets: *"Is that a baby or is that Danny DeVito?"* Whatever the meaning of the dubious phrase "all boy," Henry is it. Born three pounds two ounces, he's now twenty-five pounds and already has a gut; he looks like one of those guys who smash beer cans on their foreheads. He is loud and obnoxious, athletic and mechanical, chatty and curious, and deeply, profoundly affectionate. I just know he'll be one of those annoying men with a million opinions on how to "handle" women, and will be walked over by every last one of them.

Augustus is tiny and dark and watchful, his eyebrows knit into an expression of permanent concern. Even as a tiny infant, Henry never heard anything but "What a sweet boy!" whereas invariably people think Gus is a girl: I can dress him like rough trade on Castro Street, and still strangers stop and coo, "Isn't she adorable!" Despite a daily diet of avocado, rice pudding, and bacon, at one year old Gus barely tips the scales at fifteen pounds. He didn't crawl until last month and is still entirely uninterested in walking or even standing. He observes Henry's struggles with cool disdain, as if to say, "Land's sakes, man, what are you doing? If you just sat down, you'd find people are willing to carry you everywhere." We have realized, much to our chagrin, that we picked entirely the wrong name for him. He is not an Augustus. He is not august in any way, though of course few one-year-olds are. And though he is full of joy and good cheer he is not a hail-fellow-well-met, a guy's guy, like you'd expect a Gus to be. He is a Hugh, a Noel, or even the name I originally wanted, Alistair, which at the time prompted my cousin Amy to say, "Why don't you just pin a sign on his back that says, 'Please kick the shit out of me' and get it over with?" (For seventy-nine bucks and a lot of paperwork, you can change a baby's name. We're still thinking about it.)

Augustus is music-loving, much to his opera singer father's delight. Whereas Henry's only interest in music is taking the CD player apart, Augustus will listen to a Beethoven sonata from beginning to end and cry when it's over. He is painfully sweet but formal. Whereas Henry attaches himself to your body like a limpet, Gus bows his head to be kissed on the forehead. In a few years people will be kissing his ring.

Henry is not happy unless he has an audience and likes nothing more than to be asked to perform his little tricks and stunts. Augustus, who prefers his own company to any other and happily plays by himself for an hour, increasingly reminds me of the frog in that famous Warner Bros. cartoon. When a down-on-his-luck fellow finds an amazing performing frog, he tries to sell it to various talent scouts. The frog sits there placidly and croaks. The moment the talent scout leaves, the frog dons a top hat and spats and bursts into song. And so my son: when guests are over, he'll stare at me blankly if I try to get him to clap hands or wave. The moment they're out the door, he's practically waving semaphore flags.

Parents pray their kids will be kind and loving and loyal to each other. The concern among parents of twins is even greater, because twins are forced by circumstance to spend so much time together and to compete for their parents' attention so baldly. I look at Henry and Augustus and worry. They seem so different now, and they're only a year old. Will they be able to go to the same school? Will they be able to share friends? Will they even *like* each other?

This morning I left the room for a few minutes, and when I came back two heads—one small, one like a baby beluga—were bent over the same book. They were turning the pages together. Of course the book was upside down and they were ripping the pages, but that was not the point. My heart fluttered with happiness and with hope.

Then Henry snatched the book away and Gus bit him on the leg.

I watch and wait.

September 29, 2002

I have now owned the apartment above me for six months. Six months is enough time for me to realize that it cannot continue to be what it is now, the world's most expensive toy chest. Something must be done if my plans to live in palatial splendor in Manhattan—and by "palatial splendor" I mean "more than one bedroom"—are to be realized. So today I signed the contract with Salvatore. Salvatore is a tall, imposing man in his late fifties with deep-set granite eyes, slicked gray hair, impressive jowls, and a perpetually pained expression. The architect George's whispers of his past make heavy use of the word *famiglia*. There's recent tragedy too: a wife and only child gone, a heart that aches, or at least doesn't pump blood like it used to. When we meet, Salvatore is hiding, underneath his black cashmere overcoat, a device that monitors his heart rhythm.

John has fallen in love with Salvatore. One just has to look at the cut of his coat to know he'll do clean, precise work, and do it quickly. There's a clause people tell me to put in the contract, whereby the contractor is penalized if work isn't finished by a specific time. But fortunately here it's not necessary. I think we would insult him by asking about it, and besides, he doesn't need more pressure in his life. He has given us his word that the job will be finished in six weeks. He sees how we're living. I'm sure he understands. By Thanksgiving I'll have enough room to hold dinner for my whole family here.

I hand Salvatore the first payment of $25,000 and we shake on the deal, my hand swallowed in his.

September 30, 2002

Dr. Deneuve is lovely, but in the course of today's visit she informed me 1) we'll send Gus to a pediatric gastroenterologist and give him more blood tests to make sure nothing's wrong with his thyroid but *don't worry* we've done this before and it's been fine, and 2) Henry has a heart murmur and it sounds like nothing but *don't worry* we'll just send him to a cardiologist, and 3) Henry's head which was at the ninetieth percentile and is now at the ninety-seventh could be a sign of hydrocephalus so we'll have to watch it but *don't worry,* we'll check again at his eighteen-month visit and anyway, that sometimes happens to kids during a growth spurt.

So of course I'm not worrying.

Fear of litigation, of not explaining every horrific possibility, has ruined medicine. Where are the doctors we had as children? The ones who, if you came into the office with a spike through your head, said, "Eh, it's nothing, a couple of aspirin will clear that right up." That's the doctor I need.

October 1, 2002

So happy Gus is finally eating. I feel he is a generous person too: as much as he loves Cheerios, he methodically drops some of his on the dog, who then forages for them in his own back fur.

I worry a little about the pacifiers, though. Gus goes to bed with a pacifier in his mouth and one in each hand. Sometimes I wonder if he juggles them in his sleep. I know I should do something, but I can't. He loves them too much. My hope is that shame will make him conceal his use of them for a few years, until they become socially acceptable again when he starts attending rave parties.

October 5, 2002

I came home to find my apartment upstairs reduced to a pile of rubble and a snarl of wires where they started shifting around the electrical outlets. This is good! Renovation finally under way! I got this message on my answering machine.

Beep. Judith, this is Ultimo Construction calling. Salvatore just wants you to know the men will be finished by tomorrow, everything's under control, and the demolition went well. A few of the materials you requested may not be in stock, so there could be a slight delay. But don't worry, we're on schedule. Full speed ahead!

October 7, 2002

So pleased to find John singing to Henry and Gus this evening—Osman's aria from Mozart's *Il Seraglio. Ha! Wie wil ich triumphfieren:* "I shall triumph when I can lead you to the torture place and tighten the garrotes 'round your necks . . . and then I will have peace."

I know this doesn't sound too promising, but it's a little more soothing in German.

Gus loves it, but Henry is a little more enamored of the popular stuff. Right now he's in the living room, swaying to the beat of "Free to Be . . . You and Me," the 1970s recording by Marlo Thomas I always think of as "Free to Be . . . a Big Fat Queen." William Wants a Doll! It's OK to Cry! Housework Is Awful Unless Mommy and Daddy Do It Together! *Shut up shut up shut up!* I'm as PC as the next person, but by the time I've listened to Alan Alda for the thirtieth time, I'm ready to go out and buy Henry and Gus little toy hand grenades.

October 19, 2002

Two weeks have gone by since the renovation wrecking crew came and left. A wall is down, and there's a Dumpster up there full of debris, but no guys. What gives?

October 20, 2002

Harrowing day. Note to self: Don't put down cup of hot tea between one-year-old and husband, because one-year-old will get to it first. Gus has a burn that looks like the continent of Africa on his right thigh, and three sad little red fingers. Thank God no blisters even, just an emergency visit to the pediatrician and lots of salve. But I was shattered, and every time John tells the story, Gus becomes more and more damaged. By tomorrow I will have burned his leg off.

Still, John is the Man in an emergency. By the end of the day, when I leave to take the dog out, John is rubbing Vaseline on Gus's thigh and has covered all ten of Henry's pudgy fingers in tiny Band-Aids. Not that there's anything wrong with Henry, but John knows he wants some attention too.

October 21, 2002

Last night John dreamt I coldcocked Augustus with the butt of a gun. It's gratifying when your husband has confidence in you. I will be hearing about the hot tea for the next ten years or on John's deathbed, whichever comes first.

October 25, 2002

"I wonder what they'll be like at thirty?" John says, as Henry tips a bowl of yogurt over his head. "I'll never know of course." He shovels more rice pudding into Augustus, pleased at his tiny son's sudden huge appetite. "Every day you become bigger and stronger while every day your father becomes more decrepit."

If I'm at an age that's iffy for new motherhood, John's situation is downright surreal. Little did I think that because of these circumstances, Strom Thurmond would become my personal beacon of hope. "Hey, Strom had his last child at seventy-one, and he was around to watch his thirty-year-old son become U.S. district attorney of South Carolina!" I exclaim, as I have almost daily for the past six months.

John looks at me thoughtfully as he swallows his saw palmetto. "When they're thirty you'll be seventy—an old lady," he adds with relish. "It will be nice for you, having your boys around. You've got to take good care of yourself though, because you don't want to become dependent on them when they're too young for the responsibility."

Why, thank you for summing up all the things I fear most in one tidy conversation!

October 27, 2002
Managed to get out of the house last night to a Halloween party of magazine people. Feeling as sexless as I do, I'm always grateful when a bona fide heterosexual makes an effort to impress me. This one was plain, with a large mole on one cheek; I wanted to tell him to have it looked at. He was a lawyer in his mid-fifties, on his first divorce. He had three children, all currently living with him and hating their mother, who'd run off with her son's therapist. AJ had had too much to drink—enough that, even after he fake-guessed my age ("twenty-eight, right?" and was shocked, shocked! that I was older) and I quickly told him I was married, he continued to want to talk to me.

"You don't know what a happy person you are," he says. "I was a forever guy. I don't think there is a forever anymore."

His date roars up to us. "AJ, we are fucked, *fucked,*" she cries. Angelina has a red wine stain down the front of her Prada tuxedo; her hair must have looked lovely about three shades of blond ago. "They've lost our coats," she continues. "Mine cost three thousand dollars. We are *fucked.*"

"No," he says quietly. "'Fucked' is when you need an

organ transplant and they don't have the organ. This is a coat." I begin to like him.

He gets up to help the by-now hysterical Angelina, who is screaming inches away from the face of the hatcheck girl. "This woman is thirty-four years old and she will never have children, and she will never know what it is to love or be loved," he whispers to me, and leaves.

When I get home a half-hour late, John storms out the door, beside himself that I was out until 10:30 and he had to baby-sit his own children.

I do have other options, I think coolly. It is not the best time for John to be angry at me.

October 30, 2002
It was stupid to give that guy from the party my email address. He must have a lot of time on his hands. But the delete button is my friend.

October 31, 2002
"Real Christians don't celebrate Halloween, you know," Orma tells me, as I wrestle Henry into his bee suit. "It's a holiday for the Devil." "Yes, and for us devil *Jews*," I don't say but think in her general direction. Instead I just nod, adjust the cigar in the mouth of my skeleton, and crank up the recording of howling wolves.

I've spent the last two days trying to get Henry to say *bzzzzzz.* But we seem to be stuck on *brrr-brrr-brrr,* so now I'm telling everyone he's a *cold* bee. Gus is Eeyore, and thanks to the lugubrious cast of his sloping eyebrows a more perfect Eeyore one could not hope to find. I resisted doing what my cousin Laurie suggested, which was to dress him in a plaid shirt, tan corduroys, and little black horn-rimmed glasses and have him go as Woody Allen. Maybe next year.

As we marched through Washington Square Park, I noticed the six- and seven-year-old boys were all Spiderman and the girls were all Britney Spears, complete with low-slung pants and tiny halters and faux microphones attached to their heads. What is wrong with people? I think next year I'll send Henry and Gus out as Chippendales dancers.

Henry, greeted by the coos of admiration from strangers, seemed to enjoy his killer-bee suit despite the deep indentations the antennae made on either side of his skull. He lounged in his stroller like a wee fat pasha, awash in the love of the common man. Gus was less happy being Eeyore. I don't know if he was so upset because the Eeyore suit was too hot or because, as John suggested, he was completely humiliated. But he was that much funnier for looking Eeyorishly miserable. Marjorie's daughter, Josie, was a most stately cow. Every now and then she'd look up from the cookie she was chewing and solemnly declare, "Moo." We stopped at

Starbucks and a French woman made a fuss over Henry and
Gus but for some reason didn't notice Josie. "Fucking frog
whore," Marjorie muttered under her breath. "Fucking
surrender at the fucking drop of a hat, fucking Vichy fucks."

We met up with John, and Josie demonstrated her
"Moo," as well as her "Boo!" "Wow!" and "Bye-bye!" By the
time we got home, John, feeding Gus and Henry in their
high chairs, couldn't leave the subject alone. "Why don't
you morons talk?" he shouted. "*Brr-brr-brr,*" Henry said.

November 1, 2002
No renovation guys. No bathroom, kitchen, bedrooms,
laundry room. Just a Dumpster, a pile of rubble, and a
mortgage.

November 3, 2002
Last night, 9:30 P.M. I call my friend Annette. I know this
doesn't sound terribly late, but 9:30 is the older-mother
equivalent of calling a single girlfriend at 3 A.M.

Annette knows the code of crisis. "Judith! How are you?
What's wrong?"

"Does Thea know where her nose is?"

Concern turns to deep suspicion. "Why do you want to
know?"

I am elated.

Annette's daughter, Thea, is a year old, virtually the same age as my sons. Both her parents are professors at NYU. She is a very smart little girl. I have heard about her enormous, fifty-word vocabulary, how she distinguishes between Laa-Laa, Po, and Tinky Winky with ease. She is adorable. I hate her.

A day earlier, someone had told me Henry and Gus should be pointing to and identifying their body parts by now. When I asked them to point to their nose, they both looked at me as if I'd said, "Define $e=mc^2$."

If Thea had been able to point to her nose I would have heard about it for the next half-hour. In truth, I'd never heard Thea point to any body part. But in Annette's version of events, Thea would have not only been pointing to her nose but giving a lengthy discourse on its function, on breathing, and on the role of oxygen in sustaining life. Instead there is silence. My heart stops fibrillating. Maybe Henry and Gus are not so behind in the baby Olympics.

I am ashamed of myself. I don't mean embarrassed in a funny, ha-ha, mothers-are-competitive-what-can-you-do way. I mean *ashamed.* Before having kids, I would ceaselessly mock my friends who could talk endlessly about little Joshua who was rolling over at three months, the ease with which Sophie was handling her own bottle, or Luke and his amazing ability to pull up on furniture when other children were barely able to balance on all fours. And now here I was,

combing the Internet the minute the kids went to bed,
Googling words like "body part" and "point" and "nose."
And, most important, "developmental delay." All the while
there's a CNN-like tape scrolling on the bottom screen of
my consciousness: "Remember, your children are boys. Boys
are slower. Your children only weighed three pounds at
birth. They were six weeks premature. They were twins.
Twins take a while to catch up. Boys are..."

The last time I was this obsessed with what my peers
were doing I was in my new freshman hall at Wesleyan,
canvassing the halls to determine whether I was the only
virgin left. I was not so subtle. "*Hi! Nice to meet you. Have you
had sex yet?*" I had to know. And again, now, I had to know:
were my sons the only ones who didn't point to their noses?

Where does it come from, this wild obsession with
developmental milestones? After all, if you ask any
pediatrician or child psychologist or even those annoying
yentas who wrote *What to Expect When You're Expecting,* it
turns out there is a rather huge time window for a baby to
develop certain abilities and still be within the range of
"normal." And as far as I can tell (and trust me, I've looked),
there is no correlation between, say, "ability to clap hands at
six months" and "future career as Supreme Court justice."

As disgusted as I am with myself, I can at least say
truthfully that my anxiety doesn't stem from a fear about

my own intelligence or lack thereof. (The last time I checked, I could locate my nose.) The problem is that a baby is a tabula rasa of possibility the moment it is born. But if a mother is cursed with a certain fearful, the glass-is-half-empty temperament, every milestone not reached at the earliest possible moment can seem like a door swinging shut. In other words, the assessment "My baby still doesn't have a good pincer grasp at eleven months" very speedily becomes "Looks like he can kiss that career as a Yankee shortstop goodbye." We all want to know our children can grow up to be anything they want. Since I'm utterly unathletic, the fact that Gus is tiny and didn't even start crawling until he was a year old doesn't really bother me . . . until I start thinking, "*Well, what if his lifelong dream is to become a basketball player?* What then?"

The other problem comes when our expectations about our children come into conflict with our own family myths. My parents always told me I started speaking when I was six months old and produced short full sentences when I was a year. Meanwhile I am trying to decide if I am within my rights to chalk up another vocabulary word for Henry at thirteen months when he says "ba" for "ball"—as compared to "ba ba" for "bottle." If I was such a chatterbox, why aren't they?

Finally I call my aunt Alberta, my mother's sister, who is the family reality check. At this point I am barely coherent, so exhausted am I from screaming *"Where's your nose?"* at my children for the last forty-eight hours. I ask her to describe my astounding early language skills. "Your mother was delusional," she tells me. "You were saying something like 'pla pla ta ta sssssssss' and your mother swore you were saying 'Please pass the salt.'"

I call my mother. "Your aunt's crazy! Of course you were saying 'Please pass the salt!' You were so adorable! You had such good manners!" Did I know where my nose was when I was one year old? "I'm sure you did! I told you all about breathing, and you breathed loudly."

And that's when it dawned on me. My mother was Annette, and I'm all the better for it.

When I was a baby my mother just *knew* I was brilliant, and no one could tell her otherwise, just as she thinks her grandsons are brilliant today. She has no idea what I'm worrying about, because in Frances' World, Henry and Gus do all sorts of things they can't, in fact, do. She swears they're talking when I put them on the phone when what they are doing is yammering and drooling copiously. Random movements are to her as choreographed as ballet. A few months ago Gus put his finger in his nose—something I'm afraid he was then doing about every thirty seconds— and my mother said, "He's so advanced! He's *exploring!*"

So today when I said to Henry, "Where's your nose?" he

put his hand over his face. Hey, that's the general *direction* of the nose! Then Gus grabbed *my* nose.

Aren't they the cleverest boys?

November 5, 2002

I brought the guys to my friends' housewarming yesterday and was immediately seized with fear when I saw the cream carpet and pristine sofas and steel-and-glass coffee tables. Fortunately the only person who spilled anything on the carpet was not related to me.

When are children supposed to have separation anxiety? They were passed around from stranger to stranger and just looked around curiously at everything and smiled, showing not the slightest concern that their mother was off in another room discussing that fabulous piece in the *Styles* section about New York's best dog spas. Should I be worried they're *not* worried?

Henry was unusually merry, and I soon found out why: he was surreptitiously grabbing the glasses of booze lying around the place and slurping down the remnants. It took me a while to realize this, and by the time I did he had grabbed someone's purse and was wearing it over his head like a lampshade.

John used to like coming to parties with me, if only to complain afterwards about how politically wrongheaded everyone was. Now I go alone. It's as if, having informed me at the get-go that a life with children would be difficult, he'll ensure it's as fun- and romance-free as possible. John hates to be wrong.

Can't sleep.

Roland—now there was a guy who understood romance, I thought, as I Googled at two in the morning. I wonder what happened to him? We met in a Renaissance literature class at Columbia. He introduced himself by giving me a copy of the poems of Catullus. In retrospect I should have paid a little more attention to his choice of poet, with his paeans to manly love, his exhortations to young bridegrooms to "give up your old pleasures" and "unlawful joys."

But at the time I didn't care. He was divinely pale, compact, and beautifully sculpted. Naked, he reminded me of Michelangelo's David, if David had worn tiny wire-rim glasses. He worked as a chef to support himself through graduate school. He plied me with cheap wine and fine literature; in class, he'd whisper endearments in Italian; he'd drop by at midnight just because he wanted to see my face, he said. And then he would leave. Perhaps the leaving should have told me something too.

At the time I did wonder about why he didn't like to be touched, and particularly on his neck. Was there any truth to his story about finding his first wife strangled in a field, her murderer never found? Or was that strictly for my benefit, to inflame my already overheated imagination? No matter. I applauded his values, loved how close he was to his mother, his sister, and especially his best friend. Roland loved him so much we never did anything without him. Just once I would have liked Roland to look at me with the adoration he reserved for Glenn.

The more rejected I was, the more sure I was I could fix the problem if just given a chance. I spent one night camped outside his apartment, wrapped in my sleeping bag, slipping notes underneath his door.

He's a professor now, at a community college. Married a few times, I've heard. I tried reading a selection from one of his books online:

> *The binding relationship between the recognition of charisma and its validity fosters what might be called a systemic mutuality in charismatic groups....Significantly, this systemic mutuality has its roots in the first explicit text on charisma, Saint Paul's 1 Corinthians 12. Explaining the function of the charisms (Greek charismata gift of grace) in the congregation of...*

OK, maybe there was more than one reason we didn't stay together. He always said he loved kids, though. If he had them, they probably spent their summers in Tuscany with him. And Glenn.

November 6, 2002

Beep. Judith, this is Ultimo Construction calling. Salvatore says the kind of flooring you ordered may take a little longer than we originally anticipated. It should be here in six weeks, eight weeks tops. But there's a little problem with your building's architectural drawings. Turns out that place where we said we'd put a door? Turns out there are eight pipes running through that wall, not one. So let's figure out where else you might want a door.

November 7, 2002

Henry's gone from the usual few words necessary for survival (*baba, mama, dada, nana* for Orma) to trying to figure out everything in the house, or at least everything that begins with *b, d,* and *l* (those being, I guess, the easiest to pronounce). So there's *dog, door, ball, bubbles, book, leaf, lamp,* etc. He only gets the first half of the word, then repeats it, with a question mark, endlessly: "Do? *Do?*" What amuses me is that in between the recognizable words is a rich universe of gibberish, said in declaratives, italics, questions, and exclamations. And it's usually said about three inches away from my face. He reminds me of a foreign tourist desperately trying to make me understand *something*—whether it's that he needs directions to the Met or the fact that he's having a heart attack, I don't know.

Gus is still pretty much the Gary Cooper of babies, but he does imitate sounds. He heard a siren go by tonight, and his impression was dead-on. Being a city child, he'll no doubt soon be doing car alarms, garbage trucks backing up, buses emitting exhaust, and public spitting.

November 10, 2002

When John and I talk today, I tell him that when he returns from England I may have to take a short trip to do a cover story on a new sweet young thing out in L.A. I'd be gone no more than two days, three days tops.

"Who'll be taking care of the children at night?" he says.

"Their father?" I venture.

"Now, you know that's impossible," he says.

Do I need him for money? No. Do I need him for help with the children? No. For emotional support? Ahahahaha! So what am I doing here?

November 11, 2002

Widowers. I like older men anyway, and there's nothing sweeter than a grieving man. I scan the paper for interesting memorial services I could attend: "At the blueness of skies and in the warmth of summer we remember her. We remember her as long as we live as she is a part of us." Hm. He's not Wordsworth, but he has a certain lyrical quality.

Steven used to be an oncologist before he burnt out on death; he told me that very often the first thing the grieving partner wanted to do when the spouse died was go out and find someone to have sex with. It was an affirmation of life. I could be very good at helping the right person affirm life, I feel.

November 15, 2002

Gus, who has decided that learning to walk before he turns five might be a good idea, is at thirteen months finally deigning to pull himself up on the furniture. But he continues to torture me by not doing anything Maureen the developmental teacher asks of him. Today at the end of her bimonthly session I get another little lecture about the "homework" we need to do together: "You must teach him to find things that are partially hidden." Apparently the ability to find things that are peeking out from other things is an important developmental milestone. When Maureen hides a toy under a towel in the most obvious, look-at-me-I'm-a-toy-under-a-towel manner, Gus cocks his head, smiles pleasantly, and looks around for another toy. The dog, who is exceedingly stupid even by the embarrassingly low standards of a golden retriever, could find that toy. Why can't my son?

The things he does all day, *all fucking day,* he will not do for her. After being given the Stanley Kaplan course in body parts, he now gleefully shows off his fingers, head, and feet on command, but will he do it for Maureen? No, he will not; he will just smile. Will he ask for rice pudding or Cheerios? No, but he will grin like a Cheshire cat at a distant point over her left shoulder. Will he find the monkey, the jaguar, the lion, and say the words? Oh, no sirree, but he will smile and clap! Meanwhile, Henry is body-slamming this woman in an effort to get her attention. "Evaluate me! Evaluate me! Up! Down! Watch me put this circle piece in the puzzle! I can do the triangle too! Go ahead, ask me to get the *red* circle! I know red! You want singing? Listen to this: Lalalalalalalalala. *Hat!*"

It's 2 P.M. and I need a drink.

Maybe I'm wrong in thinking Gus doesn't like her. Maybe he likes her so much he wants her to continue showing up here and hiding toys for him for the next twenty years.

November 16, 2002

Henry has a cold, and he's being a big baby about the whole thing. Augustus, tiny as he is, is usually quite stoic about physical discomfort. Henry complains loudly and endlessly.

But it is sweet, the cantaloupe head resting on my shoulder. Occasionally he raises his head, fixes me with a very serious look, and says something in that baby porpoise language. I say, "What?" and he repeats the exact same thing, only more emphatically, furious that I'm not getting it. Then when it's clear his mother is too dense to understand, he lapses into soft moans.

In his effort to label things, Henry is constantly pointing and making the Homer Simpsonesque query, "Doi?" The other day he did this with a little naked statue of a man I have on the wall. Without thinking I said, "That's art," and then he practiced that word under his breath for a while. "Aht? Aht." The next day after his bath, he saw himself naked in the mirror, pointed at his penis, and exclaimed excitedly, "*Aht!*" It was then I realized it wasn't exactly the whole statue he had been focusing on. I started to correct him, but then I thought, "What the hell." If he's like most men I've known he'll spend the rest of his life thinking of his dick as a masterpiece anyway. "Yes, honey, that's art," I said.

November 21, 2002

I know people miss their children terribly when they're away. I know other people are calling home every ten minutes to make sure they don't miss a minute of what little Joey said, ate, did. I know all that.

Still, *wheeeeeeee.*

I'm in L.A. to interview a ravishing new actress, who is already fed up with the press. I didn't mind the twenty-four-hour wait by the phone in the aggravatingly attitudinal standard hotel, with its fuzzy video installations, shag rug on the ceiling, and bored performance artists striking poses above the front desk. I didn't mind that she was rumored to be very unforthcoming, what with the twenty handlers and the famous boyfriend and the Scientology. I *did* mind that she could barely speak English and wouldn't admit it, nixing my suggestion for the translator.

But at least I'm here on the set of a movie shoot and not locked in my apartment listening to Orma chastise me about not dressing the boys warmly enough.

November 22, 2002
Twelve hours in Las Vegas for one quick story about the Bellagio spa, and I know there's no need for me to return, ever. "What's there to do in this town if you don't drink, gamble, or go with hookers?" I muttered to the cab driver. He gave me a long, lugubrious look and said nothing; the next thing I knew, I was parked outside a church. "Meeting starts in about five minutes," he said. He handed me a sheet of the local AA schedule and a small Bible. "Day at a time," he said, before he drove off.

I got into another cab, asked the driver to take me to
Dream Car Rentals, rented a Porsche convertible, and headed
for the desert. The clouds were streaks of violet and cotton
candy, and as the sun set in the vast desert sky I listened to
Joni Mitchell's "Hejira" and wondered where I'd go next.

It was the only time in my life I ever enjoyed a drive.

November 24, 2002

There is a way to kill my entire family and get away with it.
The defense is "extreme provocation." It formed the basis of
an episode of *Law & Order,* so it must be true.

John had decided he wouldn't come to Thanksgiving.
Instead he would keep my uncle Albert company at the
nursing home. Uncle Albert was too frail to join us. I
wanted John to come with me—Sarah, the director of rehab,
was staying with Uncle Albert, despite the fact that this was
her day off—but how churlish would I look, insisting he
help me instead of staying with my uncle? So Jackie came
with me. At least no one at Amy's would ask her how long
she'd been working for me.

With my own family, it wasn't one individual thing. It
was more of a cumulative effect, starting with the two-and-
a-half-hour ride to cousin Amy's house in Scarsdale in
bumper-to-bumper traffic, where at any given moment
either Gus or Henry was screeching. Both had a stomach flu,

and true to form it affected them in different ways: one's issue was input, one's was output. Though I gave myself one and a half hours for a forty-five-minute ride, I was still an hour late, yet the food I'd brought—food that Monty had surreptitiously been trying to lick for the entire ride—was frozen solid. The reason I was bringing most of the side dishes to someone else's Thanksgiving dinner was that Amy is a reluctant chef. She has the most beautiful place settings, but she's a little hazy about what to put on them. That morning I'd gotten a call at 7 A.M.: "Judith, do you have a recipe for turkey?"

Anyway, OK, frozen food: no big deal; bring on the microwave. Only my cousin's microwave was apparently bought the year they were invented. This thing would take an hour to melt a stick of butter, much less enormous troughs of cauliflower gratinée and sweet potato pudding.

So while the turkey was burning and the side dishes were thawing and I was being blamed, Henry and Gus, now happily ensconced in Amy's House of Lethal Activities for Children, proceeded to find new and enterprising ways to destroy the place. I probably should not have praised Henry so fulsomely the first time he threw a ball over his head (Developmental milestone reached before eighteen months! How advanced!), because now he thinks a) everything bounces, and b) everything bounces really well if it's thrown over your head. So there was a great deal of time spent rescuing plates, vases, glasses, and silverware moments before they were flung in the air. He came close to harpooning Gus with a fork at one point, though Gus might not have noticed as he was intent on climbing three unusually steep steps up from the sunken living room, and he could only make it to the second one before slowly sinking to his knees, hiding his head in his hands and sobbing in despair.

When Henry wasn't hoisting wineglasses, drinking from them, and sputtering as the contents poured into his eyes and down his shirt, he too was scaling the staircase. The difference is that he gets up easily, but his new skill, coming back down, is still a work in progress. So Henry's internal dialogue went something like this: "I'm up the stairs! I'm down the stairs! I'm up the stairs! I'm down the stairs! I'm up the stairs! I'm—*aaaaaaagggggggghhhhhhhhh.*"

While all this is going on, and everybody is chatting amiably and paying me no mind, Amy is periodically calling me to the kitchen with "Hey, how do you make gravy?" and "Do you know where the potholders are?" (Of course, Amy, I can pinpoint them! This being maybe the third time I've ever stepped foot in your house.) Dinner is now an hour and a half late, and the guests (yes, there were strangers and their eerily well-behaved children at this event) finally went to their house down the road and *brought over their microwave.* What I saw, when I could find five seconds to peer in the kitchen, was Amy standing around waving her hands helplessly and this lovely, slightly bewildered Indian couple cooking dinner.

Need I go on? Do I really need to mention the incident when someone let Monty into the house, and within seconds he Hoovered an entire slab of Camembert off the coffee table? I have no idea how dinner was, because I had to protect Henry and Gus from the ravages of Amy's adorable but impervious six-year-old. Every time I turned my back she was doing something like balancing Gus precariously on the edge of the sofa to watch television. At least I didn't have to worry about any of the other kids messing with Henry, because he's so fat they couldn't lift him. "He waddles," my mother pointed out helpfully. "Do you think the doctor should check his hips?"

("Don't they all waddle?" I wondered. The other day I opened a pack of cookies in the playground and suddenly I got the attention of every fifteen-month-old. A bunch of them came lurching toward me and I had a feeling I was in a scene from *Night of the Living Dead.*)

I should add that Jackie came with me, and without her I swear one or both of my children would have killed themselves. At the end of the evening Jackie, easily the most serene person I know, said, "Wow. That was bad."

Henry and Gus cried the whole way back.

November 27, 2002

What did I do before I had children? I know I did something. But what was it? Reading: there was a lot of that. I used to read the *New York Times Book Review* to check what other people thought of the book I'd just read—not, as I do now, to have a kind of *Monarch Notes* to what the rest of the world is talking about, so that on the increasingly rare occasions I get out of the house I might be able to hold a conversation about books that did not include the words "Hop on Pop." Let's see . . . I know I cooked. Can't do that anymore, at least until the renovations are done. Right now, the way the cribs are situated in the elevated living room in this apartment, they overlook the dining table, which means we can't have dinner even after the children go to bed because they watch us. On a couple of occasions we've resorted to draping their cribs with towels so they can't see out, the way you cover the cage of a canary.

I also used to go to the movies a lot . . . four, five times a week. Do I tell myself it doesn't matter I never go now because there's nothing worth seeing, or in fact was there nothing worth seeing then and I still had a great time? I'm not sure. It's not that my life was one big smarty-pants Lollapalooza, but there was theater, dance, opera, the monthly visit to the Frick to wonder again how Vermeer made the light shine through his windows just so. Was that me doing those things?

And then there were parties. If you work in publishing in New York City, you get invited to the openings of a lot of stuff. (I always wished they'd have parties for the closings of all the failed enterprises, as the dominant New York City emotion is schadenfreude and why shouldn't we make it part of the cultural fabric?) I know it would be way cooler to cite my fear and self-consciousness at the many events where I was the least important person in the room, but the truth is I felt nothing of the sort. If there was no one I knew or felt brave enough to talk to, I was content to sit in a corner and watch. I've spent many happy hours sipping a cosmopolitan and eavesdropping on other people discussing their latest woes with Binky or their less-than-stellar appearance on *Charlie Rose.* I loved going to parties, though when I am Queen there will be a ban on wearing black. I think this would force about eighty percent of New Yorkers to show up to parties naked.

Do I miss that life? I do. I do. But maybe not enough. The one thing a mother can't explain to a nonmother is how her nerves can be rubbed raw with a dozen petty annoyances, yet when she crawls into bed she's kind of happy. It's something I can't even explain to myself.

November 30, 2002

John has finally left for England. I have asked him not to go away for two weeks at a time when the children are this young. "I have a family too, and I need to see them," he says. "*And what are we?*" I think to myself. But I know what he means, and I don't begrudge these visits. I love John's sister and nephew and wish I could see them too. Certainly I wish I could have the unspeakable luxury of two weeks without picking up a single Cheerio off the floor.

But it is a lot, being alone with them for two weeks, even with Orma here during the day. My own parents and cousins live only a half-hour away. But I can't yet manage taking two children on the train and—reason number 350 why I haven't moved to the suburbs—I hate driving. Always have, from the day I got my license when I was sixteen—I made a left in a right-hand lane and totalled a Corvette the man had just driven off the lot—my dreams of a decent life have always involved the words "limo service." So though I have a license, I'm frightened to drive in general and am positively terrified about driving with Henry and Gus. And—*not that I'm becoming my parents or anything—*

they're frightened of driving into the city and do so rarely. So I might as well be living in Billings, Montana.

Of course there are friends. I'd never think of asking people who don't have children to visit; that is too great a test of friendship. I remember too well my own trepidation when I had to plunge myself into the sticky, crumb-strewn universe of a friend with small children. I always needed to take a long shower afterwards. But even friends with children...I'm simply too embarrassed to be that needy: "*Hi, would you please come to my house and have an adult conversation with me? A conversation where, after five minutes, I'm not saying in an extremely high-pitched voice,* 'Aren't you a good boy? Aren't you good? Yee-di-di-di-di-di-di!'" After a couple of weeks of being alone with Henry and Gus, I find myself talking like this to the salespeople at Gucci.

Aside from my own discomfiture, Gus is bereft when John leaves. "Don't be ridiculous," John says over the phone, as Gus frantically babbles "Da-da-da-da-da-da-da-da" and tries to grab the receiver from me. "They have no idea I've gone away."

Today Gus picked up a book called *Hush, Little Alien,* which is about a father Martian promising his little son various things (sung to the tune of "Hush, Little Baby," only the sentiments are things like "If that shooting star's too hot, Papa's gonna find you an astronaut"). John reads it to him all the time. Anyway, Gus brought the book to me, said "Da-da-da-da-da-da-da-da," and burst into tears. So I had to get John on the phone quickly. Gus perked right up. John still doesn't conceive of Henry and Gus as human. Until they can talk, they're more or less pets without fur.

December 2, 2002

A bitterly cold day, but the sun was bright and the air smelled of burnt leaves and sugared almonds. So I marched to Washington Square Park with Henry and Gus, firm in my conviction that a) weather like this builds character, and b) there would be plenty of empty swings. (There was a third conviction that also proved true: the only other people out with their kids in this weather would be British.) At about the time Gus's lips were turning blue a Lubavitcher guy dressed as a Maccabean soldier in a plastic suit of armor came by, asked if we were Jewish, gave us chocolate coins, and said there was a puppet show about Hanukkah going on in his shul right now. Fingering the coins uncertainly, I said that the kids were too young, but thank you; he said, "No, they're not too young, they'll love it!"

I wouldn't say I'd been agonizing over the decision not to raise Henry and Gus within a religion. Neither John nor I grew up in deeply religious homes, though John certainly spent more time in the Methodist church than I did in synagogue. We both had a sense of ourselves culturally as Jew and Christian in dozens of little ways, yet neither of us felt certitude, or anything approaching it, about the existence of God. The great challenge of life, it always seemed to me, was living a decent and ethical and kind life *without* the certainty of heaven and hell, divine reward or punishment. But then again I would think that certainly you cannot be a thinking being in this culture without understanding the Old *and* New Testament. Certainly I needed to provide, if not the answers to life's big questions, a framework where those questions could be debated within the context of man's history.

Plus the shul would be serving latkes and doughnuts.

So off we march, and this poor man and his friend drag my double-wide stroller down a steep flight of stairs and settle us in. The lights dim; there is a hush; a stentorian voice offstage booms *"Behold the talking dreidel!"* There is a flash of fake lightning and a clap of thunder, at which point both children scream. Henry, despite being strapped in his stroller, does his Houdini escape trick and catapults himself into my lap. Cue fake Maccabean soldier and friend, who hustle us up the stairs.

Total time elapsed at Hanukkah puppet show: forty-five seconds.

I didn't get doughnuts or latkes, and now I'm on their mailing list. I'm tabling the religious education question for the foreseeable future.

December 10, 2002
Is John feeling some small measure of guilt at being away so long? These are the messages I came back to on my answering machine, after being out of the house for less than two hours:

Beep. Hi, don't forget to measure the children's heads and feet. We want to get them shoes for Christmas. Or hats. Get the tape measure and put it around the widest area of their heads. That's the area of largest circumference.

Beep. By the way, the tape measure is in my sewing kit, in the lower dresser drawer. It's on the right side of the kit. Make sure you put it back when you're finished with it.

Beep. I think I forgot to tell you: make sure you put the tape measure back. *I don't want to lose it.*

Beep. Have you ordered the light fixtures from Gregory's yet? Because it's possible the order won't come in for weeks. You just don't know. Remember to ask the store for the specs for the fixtures so we can give them to the contractors.

*Beep. Where are you? I hope you're at Gregory's, because the
more I think about it the more I think those light fixtures may
take weeks. Have you put the tape measure back?*

*Beep. I saw some lace-up boots. Do you prefer red or black? But I
can't buy them until you call me back with the measurements for the
boys' feet. Do you know how to measure them? I know I have a
foot-measurer somewhere. Look in the top right shelf of the closet....*

There were several more international calls with directions
about such pressing issues as rice pudding for Gus (where to
locate the kind he likes in Fairway) and vacuum cleaner
bags. ("You need to go to Desco's on Fourteenth Street. I
don't remember the exact address, but it's in the phone
book. That's *Desco's,* D-E-S-C...") Now, some may say that
this is a sign of a man who cares. I see this as a sign of a man
who believes that, tragically, he has married a retarded
woman incapable of measuring a child's head or locating a
vacuum cleaner bag in Manhattan.

December 11, 2002
Hanna Andersson was having a sale and I bought some
brightly colored turtlenecks, including one with purple and
pink stripes. This morning I put it on Gus. Then Orma
arrived. When I next checked on the boys later in the

morning, the turtleneck had mysteriously moved onto
Henry. "Gus can't wear it," Orma says. "Henry always looks
like a boy, but Gus looks too much like a girl already." I
went to lunch with an editor, and by the time I came back
the turtleneck was gone altogether. Orma just looked at me,
stony-faced. The rest of the day, I would occasionally hear
her muttering to herself, "No."

December 15, 2002
John has been away for an unusually long visit but will be
coming back tomorrow night. I asked him tonight if he had
missed us. There was a long pause. "I miss *you*, of course," he
said. "I miss the life we had."

Went to a party for a very bad book where everyone was
heartily congratulating the author, then sidling away to
gleefully dissect his reviews. The party was on the
mezzanine of a new minimalist hotel, one of those places
that's a riot of beige. I would have been having a great time,
simply thrilled to be out of the house after 6 P.M., if I hadn't
been worrying about the mezzanine collapsing. I don't like
high places or crowds, and I particularly don't like being in
high places *with* crowds. I reminded myself that everyone
here but me was very skinny, though the weight of self-
importance still made the collapse of the building a likely
scenario. I found a spot that was slightly elevated and stood

there. That way, when the mezzanine gave way and everyone fell, I would fall on top of them.

"Nice to see someone who really dressed up for the occasion," said a man who, like me, was hugging the wall. I couldn't help laughing; among the things I hadn't had time to do that evening was change from the clothes I had worn at the dog run. I fingered the freeze-dried liver in the pocket of my jeans.

"Well, at least I wasn't dressed by my mother," I said, noting his regulation khaki pants, navy Armani jacket, and rep tie. "How many of those jackets do you own?"

"Fourteen," he replied. "Same number of ties. The width of the stripes varies though."

He was a pleasant-looking man about fifty, six feet tall, with a thick mustache and thicker glasses, owlish horn-rims that should have been retired in 1985. Beneath the glasses his eyes were deep-set, hazel, and full of life. He was large-boned and well-built and trying very hard to look relaxed. His nails were gnawed off. He wore his shirt loosely to hide the soft belly of the aging jock. He had thick, curly hair like mine which he had been exceedingly proud of and now fretted over every time a few strands fell out. He wore boxers. I knew all these things without asking. He was very Jewish and very funny. His name was Alex. He reminded me of every guy I ever had a crush on in high school.

I realized then that I had met him years ago, when I used to write a lot about plastic surgery. He was one of the top surgeons in the city, and a media darling. Half the face-lifts in this room were probably his. He'd been recently divorced when I interviewed him but had since remarried and had a child. I don't remember what we had talked about years ago, but I did remember approving of him, because he was very fond of dogs. These days he had a black Labrador named Steve.

We talked about pets and Judaism and Monica Lewinsky, who was standing to our left. He thought she was very pretty and not fat at all. That's when I knew I liked him still. He showed me a picture of his child and his dog. He did not show me a picture of his wife.

After a while I excused myself, took a few turns around the room, then had to head home to relieve the baby-sitter. For a few hours I hadn't been anybody's mother. It was great.

Before I left, I remembered Steve. I circled back. Dr. Alex hadn't left his wall. I gave him all my dried liver.

December 16, 2002
John is back home. I wore the Victorian nightgown he brought back, and he wore nothing.

Afterwards he padded over to Henry and Gus's cribs. "They're bigger," he said, and stared silently for a while.

"Children this young, they don't miss their fathers," he added as he left.

December 17, 2002

Orma is annoyed with me again. I thought I was following her instructions when I bought a cheap plastic storage chest at Kmart, but she insists the storage chest she meant for me to buy, though smaller, was attractive. So now I either have to lug this chest back or worry that it too will mysteriously disappear.

She's also upset because I haven't gotten a Christmas tree, despite the fact that a tree around two fourteen-month-olds automatically becomes the Tree of Death. I thought I had a solution. John's sister Jean sent me an adorable, allegedly nonreligious Advent calendar shaped like a tree, with twenty-four little toys in twenty-four little pockets: every day you take a toy out of a pocket and hang it on the tree. It is so sweet, except for the fact that I discovered Henry likes to take the little toys out of the pockets and eat them. So I hung the tree well out of his reach, and he spent an hour crying under its felt branches in an agony of toy-ingesting deprivation. I felt I had to make it up to him somehow, so, perhaps unwisely, I gave him something he'd been coveting for a long time: his own electrical cord. He walked around for an hour holding it over his head saying, to the best of my understanding,

"Ooooooooooooooooo." He wouldn't part with it, and finally I had to sneak it out of his crib when he went to sleep.

I was complaining to Aunt Alberta about the chaos I was living in, the cramped quarters, the length of time this renovation was taking. She's always the right person to talk to. "I'd marry a homosexual just to get my house in order," she sighed.

December 21, 2002

Beep. Judith, Ultimo Construction here! Salvatore wants you to know he's sorry, Christmas is a rough time to get the workers and . . . anyway, things should get rolling by the beginning of the year. And it's really a shame about you having to send back the flooring, and after waiting ten weeks. Our supplier—well, what can you do? Anyway, looking forward to receiving another check. . . . Have a merry Christmas or, um, Happy Hanukkah or whatever you folks do.

December 25, 2002

Christmas morning was dark and glowering—a perfect day, by John's reckoning—so we strapped kids and dog into the car and went to my aunt Alberta's. It was a lovely, relatively peaceful day, though when I told my aunt, "Please get everything valuable out of arm's reach," she naturally interpreted that statement to mean "Please decorate your entire apartment with crystal baubles and razor-edged gewgaws."

"I wanted it to be festive for the children!" she said, and festive it was, though she might as well have littered the house with steak knives. But I was so grateful; with not a minute of sleep Henry and Gus were sweet and curious and chatty all day, and we managed not to destroy anything or have anything destroy us. I would like to award the woman who makes the Baby Einstein tapes a Nobel Peace Prize. Thanks to the hypnotic, not to say heroinlike quality of those tapes, countless parents have managed to enjoy holiday meals in peace. John was long-suffering, which was greatly preferable to his usual MO, endlessly complaining, and he scored extra points for getting us home alive in a blinding snowstorm. "Admit it, we really do have the sweetest children," I said, as Henry and Augustus chattered amiably in the back seat.

"Don't you realize that's exactly what Pol Pot's mother used to say?" John replied.

When we walked in the door both babies burst into tears and sobbed piteously for about five minutes before heaving big sighs and settling down for dinner.

I know just how they felt. It's tough having to wear your party face all day long.

December 28, 2002

So finally I remember why I married my husband. After a night of frequently interrupted sleep, I'd been having a day of seething, silent resentment, contemplating how little he does with the children, how he believes he's fulfilling all parental obligations if he buys rice pudding and feeds it, once a day, to Gus. He walked in today at noon, having gotten his beauty sleep at his apartment uptown. "So glad you decided to drop by," I snapped, then didn't talk to him for the rest of the afternoon.

By evening, when I'd pretty much reached my limit and put the no-necks to bed, Henry started crying and crying and when I went upstairs there was a Jackson Pollock of vomit on his bed and all over the rug. Now, I may have mentioned here, what, four thousand times? that I am squeamish. And actually it's pretty amazing they got to be fifteen months old without a major hurling episode. But hurl Henry did, and John just got all the bedding together and stripped the kid and cleaned the floor and put everything in the laundry while I stood there wringing my hands girlishly before finally getting up the nerve to pick Henry up by the elbows and shot-put him into the tub.

So John has redeemed himself, at least for now, and I will put up with his complaints for the next few days because he's caught a cold from the children. Which of course is my fault. Colds are anathema to opera singers, even retired ones, and despite my reminders that he doesn't have to be onstage tomorrow singing *Sarastro*, he is a tragic figure when congested. "I am an old man, and they are going to kill me off," he sputters, before downing his preferred medication, Glenlivet and potato chips.

AS IT TURNS OUT, the previous night was a delight compared to last. The heater upstairs in the children's room broke. There is nothing that pains John more than the thought of small shivering people. So while I took the dog out five times in the middle of the night (I had anticipated my fate earlier that day, when Monty Hoovered off the street a nicely putrefying Big Mac), John huddled upstairs on the couch, alternating between trying to fix a space heater which threw off sparks (Hmm, which to choose: frozen children or children going up in flames?) and throwing multiple blankets over H & G, who repeatedly threw them off again. I don't remember too much of what was said. But at some point I was screaming, *"They're not going to die and I have to sleep or else I can't deal with them,"* and he was replying, *"I have very few good years left, and this is no life at all."*

Neither of us slept at all, and the children are on albuterol for their wheezing. It's a drug that opens the small vessels in their lungs; it contains some form of adrenaline.

There is nothing more invigorating to two parents whose cumulative age exceeds one hundred than caring for two toddlers on speed.

December 29, 2002

Sent John home, drugged the dog with Imodium and the kids with Benadryl. It's me or them.

December 31, 2002

The choices on New Year's have always seemed beautifully simple: go out and pretend to have a good time or stay home drinking and feeling sorry for yourself. Thank God for motherhood. The perfect excuse to stay home and do absolutely nothing, and nobody thinks you're a loser.

January 2, 2003

I welcomed 2003 with a full-blown panic attack about money—sweating, gasping, heart pounding. In truth I don't do badly, considering I'm a freelance writer and freelance writers are generally one step above actors/models/waiters on the New York City pay scale. And I don't want to come across like one of those heinous people in a *New York Magazine* article on "surviving" in Manhattan on less than $200,000 a year, so blinded by their sense of entitlement they don't realize it's unseemly to be bitching about not being able to afford the second house in Quogue.

But what if something happens to me? I am more or less the sole support for Henry and Gus. John couldn't support them on his own. He couldn't even get public assistance, because he's not a United States citizen. Could he afford health insurance for them all? At his age? He'd have to leave New York, surely. Where would they go? What would they do?

My worries are seeping over into my dreams. Last night I dreamt about my money manager, Manny. In real life Manny has wanted to talk with me about my financial future—just a status report, though I've been afraid he is going to call and fire me because I no longer have enough money to be worth his time. At any rate, in the dream Manny calls me into his office and shuts the door. He tells me he's so sorry, but the space aliens who've been showing up at his house have made off with all my money. He tried to resist, but they had the anal probes, and besides, they were very convincing. They said it would be better for me if they handled my money from now on. They didn't leave their cell phone number.

There are two kinds of hypochondriac. One can't stay away from a doctor's office, and the other can't get herself to go at all for fear of hearing the horrible news. I haven't been to a doctor, other than a fertility guy or an obstetrician, for eight years. Must go. That'll help. Need someone to tell me I'm not as decrepit as I think I am.

January 4, 2003

"Scrapbooking!" gushes my friend Andrea, when I make the mistake of asking if she has any New Year's resolutions. "I know you write anyway"—thanks for noticing!—"but this is really something you do for your children. It's a way to remember all those random thoughts you had about them while they were growing up. You know, like all the things you think about their future, how they made you feel on a particular day...all your hopes and dreams. Today I wrote a love letter to my little one while she slept."

Andrea is chronically full of good intentions. What she doesn't realize is that it's far better Henry and Gus don't know what's going through my mind on a daily basis. Because my random thoughts usually go something like this:

I hope and dream that one day Henry will turn to me and say something other than "Ball?" When I brush Gus's hair just so, he looks exactly like Adolf Hitler. That would be such fun for Halloween! If Henry continues to be so good at climbing to the top of the bookcase then dropping himself off the bookshelf into the playpen, maybe I can sell him to someone on the boardwalk at

Coney Island, sort of like a diving donkey act. They are still very cute, objectively speaking, and I could clear up all my debt if I just sold one of them. Which would I sell? That would be tough. I bet it wouldn't take more than three phone calls to find the name of a lawyer who sells children...

Like that.

Scrapbooking: probably not for me.

January 8, 2003

It seemed so simple. I was going to register Henry in a toddler gymnastics class, 11:30 A.M., once a week, forty-five minutes, three hundred for thirteen weeks. It involved monkey bars and tumbling mats and maybe a ball pit. How many idiots would pay this much to watch their fifteen-month-old totter on a balance beam three inches off the ground?

Everyone in Manhattan, as it turns out. Registration started at 9 A.M. I got there at 9:15, confident I'd walk in and walk out. Turns out people had been lined up since four in the morning. I got the last place in the class, but I was so rattled that I ended up putting Henry and Gus on the waiting list for nursery school. One, I don't want to send them to nursery school when they're only two. And two, they won't even be old enough when school starts; the cutoff date is September 1, and they won't be two until September 25. But I found out the school allows a one-month grace period, so they just squeeze in under the line. And I choked. I am now number forty-six on the waiting list for a nursery school I don't want them to go to and I know nothing about and costs four thousand dollars for two afternoons a week.

I was telling my little story to a woman in the playground who did not, as I'd hoped, laugh off my concerns. "Oh, listen, if you get in there it'll be great. Even if it's your safety school, it's *fine*."

Safety school? Why is it a safety school? Are there other nurseries where they have, I don't know, more academically rigorous Legos and fake fruit?

"It's *sooo* funny how these schools wax and wane in popularity," the woman continued. "Why, just a few years ago First Pres was just a nursery like yours"—What was that fragrance in the air? Was it *eau de* momzilla?—"and now they're out of applications the hour after they open the phone." "First Pres" was First Presbyterian, a nursery school in my neighborhood where, as it happened, this woman's child went, and where, she assured me, I would have fit in beautifully, if only I'd called in time to get the application. "Most of these parents, you'd never even know who they are," she said, running down a list of media who's who in the city. "They're just so *nice*."

January 10, 2003

Henry never stops nattering away in that unrecognizable patois of residents from the Planet Baby. Augustus is still virtually mute. But lately I've had reason to wonder how much he understands.

John had pointed out to me that Gus, just getting over a cold, had a really bad cough (cue Gus coughing: *ahew ahew ahew*) and we should really have his lungs checked out. So I call the pediatrician immediately, and we're out the door. Gus isn't coughing and, in fact, looks fairly pleased, as John continues to lecture me about how I favor Henry, how everybody pays more attention to Henry, and here's poor little Gus with a terrible cough (at which point Gus starts hacking away), probably pneumonia, and I'm not really doing anything about it. "Look at the poor thing, he's so skinny, look at his shoulder blades sticking out, and listen to that cough (Gus: *ahew ahew ahew*), oh you poor boy . . ."

So I get in there with Tiny Tim, expecting to be buying him a nebulizer or maybe a heart transplant. Dr. Deneuve examines him: nothing. Everything clear. He did have bronchialitis weeks ago, so, she explained, he might have the occasional wheeze for a while, particularly in cold weather. But what about the cough? John asks, as Gus starts in with this pathetic *ahew ahew ahew.* Finally he stops. Dr.

Deneuve looks at him curiously. Gus beams. "Bad cough?" she ventures, and Gus makes like he's going to expel a lung.

"Um, you might want to stop referring to his *c-o-u-g-h*," she says. "He knows how to get Dad's attention."

He doesn't know the word "wheeze" yet, but if I make the appropriate sound, his gasp for air is like a creaking door in a haunted house.

January 15, 2003

The Ninth Circle: a raw wet day at home with children, the sky clenched down on the city like a filthy skullcap on the head of a mental patient. Gus has finally begun to pull himself up on furniture, which means pulling everything within reach down on his head. Henry is scaling the bookshelves. I have no room and I'm throwing three different balls in the hallway for Henry, Gus, and the dog, and Henry screams in frustration because the dog bowls him over and gets all three balls in his mouth at once. There is constant motion, a sense of everything whirring. I imagine this is what the Egyptians felt like when locusts blackened the skies.

I've finally had enough when I am struggling to give Henry a bath—which consists of having him stand still long enough to remove clothes, getting wet, slippery naked person to sit in bathtub seat, getting him to stop dumping all the bottles of shampoo into the toilet—while John sits in the bedroom reading the paper and drinking his single malt. "I'm supervising," he yells to me.

When I can't take one more minute of entertaining them, I put all the sofa pillows on the floor. This is their signal to attack each other. I watched them go at it for an hour this afternoon. Gus always wins. Henry has at least ten pounds on him, and his main strategy is just to sit on his brother or stand up and then fall back on him in that classic "Timberrrr" wrestling move. Yet somehow Gus manages to twist away, momentarily get Henry in a headlock, and bite him. Most of these sessions end with Henry, all twenty-seven pounds of him, bawling in a corner, with sixteen-and-a-half-pound Gus cackling maniacally. Then Henry scowls, grits his (four) teeth, and they start again.

I've thought of titling these events WWE Baby Smackdown, and getting them broadcast on Telemundo, with narration dubbed in Spanish. *El Psyko Augusssssssto! versus El Gigante Henry!* There will be mugs, posters, T-shirts, I think, as they scream and I down my third gimlet.

January 17, 2003

> In the great green room
> There was a telephone
> And a red balloon

And a picture of—
The cow jumping over the moon...

Henry and Gus are staring at me slack-jawed. They are, as
always, mesmerized, having no idea their mother wants to
gouge out her eyes with chopsticks. It is difficult to convey
how annoying I find *Goodnight Moon:* it set my teeth on edge
the first time, and it does not improve greatly on the four
thousandth reading. By the time I get to "Goodnight
kittens" and "Goodnight mittens" I am making up the
words as I go along. *"Goodnight Mom/Goodnight bomb/Goodnight
Mr. Bad Sadam."* "Sadaaaaam," Henry croons approvingly.
Well, at least he's paying attention.

Yet as much as I dislike the ritual bedtime reading of
Goodnight Moon, as much as I continue to be mystified by its
popularity and Xanax-like effect on wee children, it is still a
book. Which means I hate it far less than I hate almost
everything for kids on television. Every time I think I can't
read *Goodnight Moon* again, I remember Roald Dahl's poem
"Television," which begins

The most important thing we've learned
So far as children are concerned,
Is never NEVER NEVER let
Them near your television set—

Or better still, just don't install
The idiotic thing at all.

When Henry and Gus were born I had only one concrete
image of motherhood: the three of us sitting around on a
rainy day, each engrossed in a different Brontë novel. I know
they are boys. I know I'm a moron. But this is the dream I
still cling to. They would adore, like I did, having their
imaginations fed but not *spoon*-fed; they would delight in
escaping to worlds far different from their own; they would
learn how people really think and feel and act not from
"reality TV" (an oxymoron if there ever was one) or, God
help them, magazines, but from the best books.

Now, it's perfectly possible this dream will still come true.
They are, after all, only sixteen months old, and they can get
darn excited about not only *Goodnight Moon* but also *The Big
Red Barn, I Went Walking,* and, *Hand, Hand, Fingers, Thumb.*
("*Mon-kees,*" Gus shrieks at me, approximately every thirty
seconds—which, as every mother with that book in residence
knows, is the cue to shriek back, "Monkeys come and
monkeys drum, drum drum drum drum drum drum *drum.*")

But then, I look at the hold the television screen has on
them and I think, "What are the chances?"

The first grown-up, purposeful act Henry and Gus ever
learned was turning on the TV. (I have to admit I still enjoy

watching Henry do this, then climb up on the couch and settle in with a sigh. I'm always tempted to hand him a beer.) Sometimes I can convince myself they're learning something useful. The other day Henry happened to turn on the television to a professional women's soccer match. As he watched, he muttered two things to himself, over and over: "Ball!" and "Yay!" That pretty much sums up everything you need to know about sports.

Of course the powerful, narcotizing effect of television on kids is nothing new. When we were growing up there was also programming for children. Saturday morning cartoons were partially a kid's reward for a hard week at school, and partially a chance for our parents to have morning sex without the threat of interruption. (Did I just say that? *Shudder*. Naturally I do not mean *my* parents.) But thirty years ago, did the average child watch three to four hours of television every day, as an American child does now? Did we spend more hours in front of TV every year (about 1,500) than we did in class (about 900)? There is a difference between programming for kids and *entire networks set up to capture their attention and sell them stuff.* I can't get too exercised about the sex-and-violence argument, that kids are exposed to too much too soon; television is only one perpetrator of many, and our job as parents is to be counterbalances to the things we dislike in the culture. Far harder for us as parents is to explain away and deny a kid's lust for the good life, as presented by kids' television: the crap food, the toys that break in a day. The purpose of reading is to make us think. The purpose of television is to make us consume.

Every parent I know struggles with the siren call of the tube. It becomes battleground, the locus for both rewards and punishments. *"If you do X, you can watch Y":* that's the parental mathematical equation. One of the most erudite men I know lets his sons (now three and five) have television sets in their rooms; having given in early, he doesn't have the stomach to thwart them now.

I realize it is very boring and politically correct to rail against the evils of television, and in truth there are some kids' shows I love. Not surprisingly, they're the ones I grew up with: *Mr. Rogers* and *Sesame Street. Mr. Rogers,* who will hopefully live forever in reruns, is still a little too sophisticated for my kids, but *Sesame Street* is another story. I love *Sesame Street,* and sometimes I'll watch it even when Henry and Gus aren't around. As far as they know, *Street* is really the only show on television, because it's the only one so far I let them watch. It is endlessly inventive, sweet without being sanctimonious, culturally diverse without making a Huge! Big! Deal! about it. Plus the music is as addictive to adults as children. (John has taken to calling me up in the middle of the day and, without so much as a hello, whispering, "One banana, two banana, one for me and one for you banana." "Count three or four or maybe more banana," I whisper back kittenishly, "'cause banana don't grow alone." Between us these days, this is what passes for phone sex.)

So: so far, with the exception of the occasional soccer game, Henry and Gus really know only the world of videos I select and *Sesame Street.* I admit, not without a little shame, that I use the television for a few moments (OK, an hour) of respite when I need to vacuum or I just can't sing one more rendition of "Inky Dinky Spider." And every day I worry about what's right. Sometimes I think the children of my friends, parents with their resigned attitudes toward the tube, will grow up to be neurosurgeons, while poor Henry and Gus will become so obsessed with television from their early deprivation that their highest aspiration will be selling video equipment at The Wiz.

Surely my mother must have done something right to foster my love of reading, right? Recently I called her and asked. "Oh, sure, I read to you, but I propped you up in front of the televison starting when you were three months old. You seemed to enjoy it!"

So who knows what's right? I just pray that somehow they'll learn to watch as I do—occasionally and temperately—but will find their real passion in books. Even if that means not four thousand but forty thousand readings of *Goodnight Moon.*

So goodnight mama. Goodnight llama. Goodnight cave dweller named Osama.

January 20, 2003

My pediatrician is extremely conscientious and yet I want her dead. I bring in Gus, who has some little bug, and she weighs him on this scale she has problems using and he weighs little more than sixteen pounds, almost the same as he did three months ago. And this is very upsetting to me, and while she's halfheartedly reassuring me not to worry she stops what she's doing, gets this look on her face, says, "Wait a minute," and shines a light in his eyes. Then goes, "Oh, no, that's fine." And then continues her conversation. And meanwhile I'm thinking, "So when are you going to tell me about the tumor on his optical nerve that is also, apparently, preventing him from gaining weight?" At this point I've learned not to even ask her what she thought she saw. I just don't want to know.

We've been putting off any testing to find out what the problem is, but we're going to have to suck it up and check his blood thyroid levels. We'll also have to do these complicated stool tests that involve documenting every Cheerio and chicken nugget that goes into his mouth, then saving everything that exits in a bucket for three days. This test is designed to see if he isn't absorbing fat. I can't imagine this is the problem, since it would be pretty obvious to me already. Anyone who's ever had a dog who ate, say, a few slices of pizza knows what nonabsorbed fat looks like.

Another possibility is cystic fibrosis, but no one in either of our families has had it and by now you'd think we'd know if Gus did. One of the symptoms, in addition to thickened mucus and chronic lung infections, is salty skin: the genetic mutation does something to the way the body processes salt. So for the last day John and I have been frantically licking Gus's arm, then licking our own, then licking Henry (we'd probably lick the dog if he'd stand still), and I'm like, "We're *all* salty! Shit!"

Meanwhile Gus continues to have a hollow leg. He lives on mashed potato that's half butter and ground meat; cheese and avocado; rice pudding at every meal. He drinks milk spiked with cream, drinks three of those bottles throughout the night. He is brimming with energy and never skips a meal, as compared to Henry, who now weighs almost thirty pounds and eats sparingly. And Henry's a vegetarian, while Gus loves meat. It's like living with a brontosaurus and a tiny velociraptor.

I never understood what my friends would get so overwrought about when their tots didn't eat much, or only ate one food for days on end, or only ate things that were blue. But it turns out there is some inner impulse to feed, as primal and mindless as the pelican shoving predigested fish down the gullets of its fledglings. If I could guarantee it would make Gus gain weight, I'd be predigesting the fish and upchucking it myself.

February 1, 2003

Orma must go. She must. I have an article due tomorrow, not a fake deadline, a real one, and she's nagging me to take Henry to the doctor because he's crying and whiny. Hello, he has a nasty cold! He is a drama queen! No fever, throat isn't red, not pulling on ears, and *stopped crying when Irene, the occupational therapist, brought him lots of interesting new toys.*

It seems I do not safeguard my children's health, according to Orma. At the medical school she apparently attended colds are caused by the failure to dress children in four layers of clothing during the winter. Also, wet heads = death. And something too frightening to mention happens to a child who doesn't wear socks to bed.

Every morning she inspects Henry and Gus. "I see Gus isn't wearing socks this morning," she says slowly, the accusation lingering in the air. Because he pulls them off! Am I supposed to hover over his crib all night, on sock patrol? "Did you dry Henry's hair last night?" Not thoroughly enough, so I guess he'll have Legionnaires' disease today. I like warmth as much as the next person, but bougainvillea could grow in my apartment.

Henry continues to whine. Pediatrician appointment in half an hour.

HENRY ACTUALLY DOES HAVE an ear infection.

Orma is gloating.

I think I'll dress Henry and Gus in pink just to make her nuts.

February 7, 2003

Oh, the expression on Henry and Gus's faces when Orma came back from a week's vacation. I thought Gus was going to have a coronary. He still doesn't walk yet, just cruises the furniture. But when he saw Orma he was like a crippled man at Lourdes casting off his crutches: he let go of the chair he'd been clinging to, threw his arms in the air and stood alone for a full ten seconds, like, "She's back. Thank you, Jesus."

She's got to stay. She can't leave till they're twenty.

February 14, 2003

Beep. Judith, happy Valentine's Day! Salvatore wants you to know he's so sorry there have been some slight delays, so he's not passing along the extra charges he'll incur shipping your tiles

*from California. But he can't order the tiles until we receive
another check. Also, your architect told us you loved the new
wood doors, but you were wondering why they were painted
white when the wood was supposed to be stained and left bare.
Well, water under the bridge! And the flooring's beautiful,
right? So glad it finally arrived; the workers will be there very
soon to install it. Two, three weeks tops. Anyway, we look
forward to getting your next check.*

This renovation is costing about $85,000, and every month
I'm not using the apartment upstairs is about $3,500 in
mortgage and maintenance. My friend Lige has offered to
punch a big hole in my ceiling and install a rope ladder for
only $25,000.

February 16, 2003

Gus the hothouse flower does not appreciate this weather,
but Henry the cold-loving Celt trotted around the
neighborhood yesterday in his mummy snowsuit, smacking
the snowdrifts with his mittens and holding up the results
for me to see, making his all-purpose what-the-hell-is-this
sound, "Ghee?" Finally the cold and wet infiltrated the
acrylic, and that was *not fair*, so we wheeled him over to his
friend for a restorative bottle and a video.

It's funny, though, how the sibling who tortures is also the one who can't do without his brother. Gus, understandably, wishes Henry would vanish in a puff of stage smoke, like Captain Kirk on *Star Trek*. But Henry, who spends his days stealing Gus's pacifier, combing his hair against his will, and forcing him to wear a hat—Henry is beside himself with worry when Gus isn't around. If I take Henry somewhere alone all I hear is "Baby? Baby? Baby? *Baby!*" until I tell him Gus is back home and he's fine. There will be silence for thirty seconds, and then, "Baby?"

When I take Gus anywhere alone, he doesn't say much. But the thought balloon over his head is "Please God, let it be true. Let me finally be an only child."

February 18, 2003

Shattered from a day with one very sick baby and one bursting-with-health baby. It's worse than when both of them are sick, because it's impossible to get healthy Henry to understand that now is not the best time to repeatedly dump a bucket over his brother's head. Plus, when it comes to medication, it's like the old joke about pilling a dog versus pilling a cat, with Henry as the dog and Gus the cat. Henry: Give him medicine, followed by a cookie chaser. Gus: Pin him to the ground screaming as you hold his nose, shoot into side of his mouth, try to hold his mouth shut to prevent a geyser of sweet red goo from reappearing. The entire time I'm wrestling Gus, Henry is poking me and shouting, "Want, *want*" because apparently Tylenol is, for him, the fifth food group.

Gus hasn't been able to eat anything for four days, which, given how tiny he is, puts John into a panic. At the end of the day all he has is some stomach virus, but John with his flair for the dramatic is waking up in the middle of the night and whispering, "Gus isn't going to make it."

February 19, 2003

What I find touching about listening to Henry and Gus try to talk is how eager they are to participate, to be part of the conversation, however few words they have. So when John comes home at the end of the day, I feel like we're in our own Ionesco play:

Me (to John): How was your day?

Henry: Shoe!

John (to me): I went to visit Richard in the hospital.
   He's looking brighter today.

Gus: Jaguar!

Me: Do the doctors think he'll be out of there this week?

Henry: Wreath, wreath. *Ball.*

Gus: Bounce bounce bounce. *Lion!*

Very soon, of course, John and I have abandoned our conversation and are randomly shouting, "Jaguar! Shoe!" and they are then so very happy.

February 20, 2003
Henry has not mastered the intricacies of "I'm gonna get you." While Gus seems to know instinctively this is the signal to run (or in his case crawl) like the wind away from me, Henry only has to hear the phrase to come lumbering joyously *toward* me. Shamefully, I use this to my advantage. When he's running away I shout, "I'm gonna *get* you," and he does a 180, then slams into my knees.

I've noticed Gus now prefers bathing with Henry, since Henry's such an enthusiast about the whole thing. A little too enthusiastic. The other day when I turned my back for a few minutes I found him sitting in the bathtub, fully clothed and surrounded by bottles of wash and shampoo, looking up at me expectantly.

February 26, 2003
Gus passed an important milestone today: he showed the speech pathologist who came to evaluate him that he is not a 'tard. With Maureen, he is still and forever a mute; as soon as she comes and sits down next to him you can hear the crickets chirping in my apartment. But with this new

speech pathologist guy, Gus will hold forth. "Cow—moo!
Cat—miaow! Up—down, open—close. Elphant, elphant,
pig, oink—rabbit." And a rendition of "Twinkle, Twinkle,
Little Star" complete with hand gestures. (Twinkling! Arms
raised for "up above the world so high"!) I've never seen him
do this before, and I certainly haven't shown him. There's
nothing so brilliant about this, except for the fact that he
was saying all these words I never heard him say before. It
might have simply been because I removed Henry from the
scene, so for once Gus could get a word in without his
loudmouth brother shouting all the time.

Of course, as soon as the speech pathologist left, Gus
became Marcel Marceau for the rest of the evening. No
amount of oinking, barking, and whinnying on my part
could get him to utter a word. But as I was cleaning up
around his high chair, worrying and mindlessly humming
one of the dozen earworm baby tunes that float in my head
all day, I had just gotten to *"Old MacDonald had a farm"*
when Gus tapped me on the back, fixed me with a very
serious gaze, and loudly declared, *"E-i-e-i-o."*

He didn't want to be left out, poor thing.

February 28, 2003
Don't want to let another month go by without getting a
physical. Will make the appointment tomorrow. Or soon.

March 1, 2003

Playground, around dusk. Lots of seven-, eight-year-old kids and their parents milling about. A man in his early sixties, dignified, jovial-looking, sits on a park bench alone. His smile is noncommittal, his eyes are watchful. I am looking around for the child he's minding. He's not.

I am a coward and always will be. I dread confrontation. Several times in my twenties, I sat through entire movies rigid with anxiety while some guy in an almost-empty movie theater moved his seat closer and closer, then sat down next to me and made those furtive, barely perceptible movements that made me aware he was having a much better time at this movie than I was. A leg would touch mine, and there would be a soft moan. I'd never move seats. I didn't want to offend.

"Which kid is yours?" I ask. His eyes flicker in my direction. He doesn't answer me. I ask again. There is a mumble. "I'm giving you thirty seconds to leave before I call the police," I say. That gets his attention. "This is a public space," he says. "I have a right—"

"You have a hard-on," I think. But I don't say it. I can't. I just look him directly in the place that is not his eyes and say, "I really think you need to go."

He leaves. I'm still shaking an hour later.

It's not that I don't feel sorry for him. I do. Why are some people wired like this? It must be horrible to have the thing you most desire, the thing that seems most *natural* for you to want, be a crime. A hundred years ago a gay man would have received the same vilification.

But this is not a hundred years ago. This is now. These are my kids. They will not be yours, even in your dreams.

March 4, 2003

Do they make Xanax in infant formula? The children have been cowering in the living room because the renovation crew upstairs was removing, chunk by chunk, the concrete slab they had just put down in the bathroom—a slab that, as it turns out, makes it impossible for the plumber to properly hook the new toilet into the wall. A concrete slab being drilled out is a noisy affair, and Henry and Gus are going berserk. At one point I decided that if Henry understood what the noise was and where it was coming from, he wouldn't be frightened. So I brought him upstairs. Big mistake. He leapt into my arms like a stag and took about ten minutes to calm down. I've tried to distract him with Elmo and Baby Bear, but when he's not watching *Sesame Street* he's pointing at the ceiling intermittently and shouting, "Men. *Men!*" in this terrified, they're-coming-to-get-me voice. Gus is so frightened he's zoned out completely, willing himself to do nothing but stare at the television. He has a pacifier in his mouth, one in each hand, and a small pile surrounding him. I don't know where they all came from. Apparently he's been stockpiling.

March 5, 2003
Uncle Albert has not recovered significantly from his stroke. He is still entirely reliant on nursing help. He is a handsome, brilliant, broken man in a state of constant fury at his helplessness. However, he and Sarah, the rehab director, are planning to move in together. She knows he has no money. She knows he lives in a cramped studio apartment. He has nothing to offer but himself.

Which proves that if you are a man in this culture, you can be crippled, broke, old, paralyzed, and unable to speak— and still get laid. Uncle Albert makes me glad I had boys.

March 6, 2003
I've been quite jolly, having returned from my friend's son's bar mitzvah—fun, and comforting to the hypochondriac in me. (Everyone there was a doctor, so if I had a heart attack there would be ten cardiologists elbowing each other out of the way to revive me.) Then John stayed over last night, waking me up at 3 A.M. to say how depressed he was and how overwhelmed he felt. Which of my friends did especially well in her divorce? I've got to make sure I get the right lawyer.

No. I don't want to be divorced. I married the smartest,

most decent man I know. The guy who'd run into the burning building to save me (complaining all the way, but still). After twelve years, as he charges ahead of me on the street, grumbling about how slowly everyone else walks, he unconsciously thrusts out his hand behind him and reaches for mine.

But I am so sick of hearing how depressed *he* is and how his life is a misery and how trapped *he* feels. *Dude.* Maybe you should have said something the first, or no, the fifth or sixth or seventh time a nurse handed you a sterile cup and told you to produce. When you go through IVF, it's not like parenthood is sprung on you. *"What, you mean after seven years of needles and mind-scrambling drugs and invasive medical procedures and waiting rooms and thousands upon thousands of dollars, you're going to have a baby? You tricked me!"*

Plus you've got your wife working and paying for full-time help: how much easier could I make your life? Sorry I haven't shelled out for the manservant you need. Sorry I haven't opened a vein.

ONE DRINK LATER: There is that little matter of children. How bad must a marriage be, how thick with contempt and recrimination, for a woman to voluntarily sever the relationship between father and child? I used to scoff at people who said they stayed together "for the sake of

the children." That line: a lame excuse for their own failure
of will. Now I think, "You are a hero." More people *should*
accommodate themselves, even if that means a secret life, as
long as Dad walks through the door every day. Children
don't need us to be happy. Children need us to be there.

I need another drink.

I check my email. Something from that guy I met at the
book party a few months ago. Weird. Delete.

Third drink. OK, undelete.

HOW DID HE KNOW MY BIRTHDAY was coming up?
Well, certainly we know some of the same people; Alex has
more or less rid Condé Nast of its nasolabial folds. Whoever
told him about my birthday knows me well, judging by his
suggestion of getting together at Peter Luger's.

Maybe he's working on a book and needs a ghostwriter.
Or maybe he wants me to interview him. That must be it.
Even the busiest plastic surgeons are publicity hounds, and
Alex is no exception. Poor thing. Should I tell him I don't
write that frequently about plastic surgery anymore? Or
should I let him find out after he's bought me a porterhouse?
Of course I do write about it sometimes, and he's a valuable,
not to mention charming, source. I really do need to keep
up to date with what these guys are doing. I wonder what

are the latest techniques to smooth out those little crinkly lines smokers get around their mouths? Alex will know.

March 9, 2003

We use the word "innocent" to describe children so often, it's lost its meaning. We think of innocence in terms of purity, of a person untarnished by unkind thoughts or deeds. But children can be unkind, cruel even; that's not where their innocence lies. A child is innocent because she has no preconceived notions of how the world should work. Her vision is not obscured by habit.

I couldn't help but think about innocence today as I watched Henry and Gus hard at play. Gus was fiddling with some nattering electronic toy that recites the alphabet, and every time he paused for two seconds the toy chirped, "Press the button! Press the button!" I saw Henry undoing his onesie, pulling up his shirt, and pressing his belly button. Then he came over to me with a wounded look on his face, like, "What's wrong? I'm pressing the button and nothing's happening. *I must be broken.*"

March 10, 2003

Dear Supermarket Checkout Lady
    with the Vast Array of Opinions:
Undoubtedly there are many people interested in your

views on high protein, low-carb diets. But what are the chances a haggard, clearly in-a-rush mother of twins is one of those people, particularly when the twins in question are about to implode right before your eyes? Just because a person is buying a lot of meat does not, ipso facto, mean she wants to discuss nutritional theories. Yet curiously, watching one of her children rip into a sealed package of raw chuck does not seem to stop your musings. "See, I'm borderline diabetic, and high protein really keeps me balanced," you say, as you ignore the growing queue. "The genius thing about Atkins is that you're allowed some fruit. I can be totally satisfied by a mango.

"There's such a huge diet industry making billions of dollars, nobody wanted to admit that Atkins was right," you continue, as the twin who's been prevented from eating raw meat begins to cry, and the other twin reaches over to the handy nearby candy display and begins methodically tearing the wrappers off the Snickers bars. "If Atkins was right, then they'd all go out of business."

One geological era melts into another while the mother waits for you to ring up her fifteen items. The twin with shreds of raw meat still dangling from his mouth now attempts to climb out of the cart, while the one dismantling the display of Snickers bars has now turned his attention to Kit-Kats. But did the eventual paying for the items, including the six mangled candy bars, in any way signal the end of the conversation? No, it did not.

"Atkins didn't have a heart attack," you shout helpfully after the rapidly retreating figure of the mother, whose children by this time are both howling, having been cruelly denied the pleasures of raw meat and cheap chocolate. "That story was part of the diet industry's conspiracy. Remember, Atkins actually *fell down and hit his head.*"

Thanks for sharing.

Sincerely—

March 11, 2003

The boys are napping. Orma walks into my room, stands silently at the door until I sense a presence and turn around.

"Do you believe?"

I sense a trap. "In what, Orma?"

"In the Creator. You believe in the Almighty Creator, don't you?"

"Well, I'd say I'm agnostic. I haven't settled the question in my own mind."

"Oh." She leaves, as quietly as she came.

"Wait a second," I say, completely forgetting what I was writing about. "What made you ask?"

"Yvonne told me you were a deep, true believer." Yvonne: Orma's sister, and my original baby nurse.

Now I think Orma's going to quit. Would it be so wrong if I told her that if I *did* believe, I'd consider becoming a Baptist?

"This morning I thought, 'Yesterday was so hot and miserable.' Then the weather changed. So sudden! It's beautiful. That's proof for you that He is there, He is good. Isn't it?"

I smile and shrug. I wouldn't have to have these conversations if I'd just circumcised Henry and Gus. She would have just thought, "Jew, lost," and that would have been the end of it.

A half-hour later Orma came back to my room, beaming. "You're a good woman anyway," she said, and vanished.

March 12, 2003

OK. Let's say Henry and Gus move their bowels, conservatively, four times a day each. Their intestines are busy. Now I'm not with them all day, so I'm doing the changing just twice a day on weekdays, and four times each on weekends. That's twenty times during the week, sixteen times on weekends, thirty-six craps a week, one hundred forty-four a month. If they're toilet trained at three years I've only got another twenty months left. 144 (per month) x 20 = 2,280. Hey, that's not bad!

Now Monty. Twice a day, minimum. He's five now, and if he lives to be fourteen, that's another nine years. So that's 730 times a year x 9 = 9,450 defecations I will be picking up.

So, 7,850 more times I will be dealing with other creatures' shit. OK.

But.

When the dog turns fourteen and dies, John will be seventy-eight.

Depends?

"Are you still awake?" John says. "For God's sake it's 2 A.M. What are you thinking about?"

"Nothing. Go back to sleep."

March 14, 2003

Monty is just beginning to have his fur grasped by small hands that, once they hold on to something, find it hard to let go. All he does is look to me for help. Then when I scold them, wresting his fur from their grip, he goes over and gives their feet a tongue bath. If I could wave a magic wand, I'd give Henry and Gus the nature of my golden retriever.

Couldn't help thinking about Monty today, when a friend who's just had a child told me she's giving away her (perfectly lovely, gentle) dog. She says she has no time, and besides, allergies run in her family. What if her baby is allergic?

I have no sympathy. None. Monty was my child substitute too, just like Rufus was hers. And of course having Monty now in this tiny apartment is a huge PITA. (Not that it would really matter where I lived. Golden retrievers always need to be inches from their humans. I could live in Balmoral, and I'd still be tripping over him.) The babies suck up all my time, yet there's the dog who needs to be exercised, hard, at least three times a day. I have to pay Jack the dog walker to come first thing in the morning because I can't give both dog and babies my time as soon as they all wake up.

But this dog, I believe, is partly responsible for my being able to get pregnant in the first place. I owe him. A dog is a family member, even if he's a slobbering, shedding, takes-up-the-couch family member with fish breath and a single-digit IQ. Anyone who'd give up her dog would give up her baby if she suddenly got a cuter one.

March 15, 2003
"That dog smells," says Orma, for perhaps the thousandth time.

I do feel a bit worried. She gave Monty the Look. It's the look I saw the day before my bathroom rug disappeared forever.

March 16, 2003

Mornings, before Orma comes.

If John happens to be staying downtown, John pokes me in the side and mentions that the children are awake. As if I didn't know. They're both rattling their empty bottles on the bars of their cribs; they might as well be chanting, "Attica! Attica!" Get up. John rolls over for a little more sleep.

John and I are on first floor, in bedroom. Babies are on second floor, in living room. Heavily mortgaged whole other apartment is on third floor—or what will be the third floor, when it is connected to this apartment with a staircase. Staircase to third floor seems a distant, fond fantasy. For now heavily mortgaged other apartment remains unused and unusable. I have delegated dealings with Salvatore the contractor to John, and John, inexplicably and uncharacteristically, is being more foolishly patient than I've been. Life is untenable. Remind myself, with a heavy heart, that *I must call Salvatore.*

Put water up for John's tea. Put water up for my coffee. Step over dog, avoiding stuffed animals that have been hurled out of cribs in the middle of the night, and rescue babies from crib prison.

John pretends to sleep.

Change babies. John emerges from bedroom, makes cup of tea, picks up paper, goes back into bedroom, and shuts door.

If my back is acting up, as it has lately, take muscle relaxants necessary to get through a day of baby lifting. Put babies on the floor for half-hour of mayhem. Try to get Henry not to rip the new Maisy book in half. Try to get Gus not to pull over the lamp. Separate them when they grab each other's onesies and pull.

John, in bedroom on first floor, drinking tea and reading the paper.

Coax babies down the stairs, into their high chairs. Fall over dog, who has resumed his place at bottom of stairs, no matter that he's been kicked out of that spot fourteen thousand times. First thing in the morning, all you see is his nose peeking out; he's covered by the blankets, stuffed toys, and binkies the boys have thrown out of their beds on top of him. Still, he doesn't move. Have I mentioned he's not a very bright boy?

Grateful that Henry can negotiate the stairs himself, as today is one of the days I can barely lift him. Pour out Cheerios for Gus, a few crackers for Henry; cut up banana for Gus, pineapple for Henry. Scramble egg for Henry, spoon out yogurt for Gus. Pray that soon they will eat some of the same foods.

My mother calls, as she does every morning, not only to find out what's happening with the babies but to share her latest crime obsession. Today it's the murder of Laci

Peterson, the pregnant California woman whose philandering husband has already been convicted in the press as the murderer. We determine that he's Catholic, which is good; my mother's first fearful question about any homicidal maniac is "Was he Jewish?" That question settled, we discuss the possibility of Peterson's being tried and getting the death penalty. My mother always asks the questions I'm wondering about but feel too silly to say out loud. "Do you know what's amazing?" she asks. "That people on death row actually have a last meal. I mean, how do they have an appetite?"

Anna arrives, early. The problem with being the best cleaner in New York City is that you are a little high-strung. Anna doesn't just get rid of dirt; she broods about it. She believes it is killing her. Also she has many Polish remedies for life's ills, and she likes to share them with me.

"Judy, you know, if somebody has kidney stone, beer is perfect medicine," she tells me, apropos of nothing. "I'm sure because my friend is in Poland, she was drink and the stone was go out, like baby. I tell you, drink beer. Not you have to be drunk but one, two, three, beer is OK. I tell friend, he say, 'Anna, you better than doctor.'"

Anna is still explaining her new cure for her sinuses, which involves garlic, when Jack shows up to get Monty. By now Henry and Gus are shouting "*down, down*" in an effort to be sprung from their high chairs, while Jack takes a moment to discuss the sequins on a gown he saw on Bette Davis in last night's viewing of *Now, Voyager.* Jack loves the 1930s designer Irene and can describe each of her dresses in detail.

John emerges from the bedroom to have a word with Jack about the war. They commiserate about the idiocies of Bush and their mutual hope that this country will finally come to its senses while I pick up the Cheerios that have been whizzing through the air. I make a mental note to try to find a cereal the dog likes. Feeding them foods the dog likes has become my guiding nutritional principle, because if he'll eat it, I don't have to pick it up off the floor.

Jack and Monty leave. Anna is telling me something very passionately, but her accent is a little hard to decipher, so I'm nodding a lot. Eventually I realize she's telling me she just started on Fosamax for osteoporosis, and she's taking "the Paxil" for stress. John says hello to his offspring, kisses their heads, sings the ABC song, then heads to the gym, satisfied he's met his parental responsibilities for the day.

For thirty seconds I resist the idea of turning on the television set. Then I remember the battle I have getting the children into clothing without it. Television set goes on. Clothing slips on much more easily when four eyeballs are glued to *Teletubbies*. I love the *Teletubbies* and am reminded that Jerry Falwell and I have one thing we agree on: Tinky

Winky, swinging that big purse, *is* gay. But I celebrate his difference! The only bad thing about the *Teletubbies* is that now, whenever we're outside, Henry points up and asks, "Baby?" He's a little disappointed there isn't an enormous chortling baby embedded in the sun.

By the time Orma arrives it is only 8:30, and I'm exhausted. I try not to have the television on when she walks in the door because, blessedly, she doesn't approve of television and the boys don't see it on her watch. Today, though, I miscalculate. She looks at me, then looks at the television. "Boys don't like *Teletubbies*," she says, switching it off. "That's for girls."

March 27, 2003

Beep. Judith, Ultimo Construction here. We're very, very sorry about the floors. I know we said they'd be in a few weeks ago. But here's the thing. The installer? Of the floors? He died. Isn't it your birthday? I remember, because we were supposed to . . . well, it doesn't matter now! Anyway, we're looking into a new installer, and we'll let you know what's happening as soon as we know. Hope you have a lovely weekend.

March 28, 2003

My birthday. John will get me a lovely present, once I decide what it should be. He really doesn't like to surprise me; he knows we have such different tastes, and he wants to make sure I get exactly what I want. It's so sweet, in a way. But it's also a little sad. I miss surprises.

We had lunch at my new favorite southwestern place. I thought John wouldn't hate it too much because it wasn't outrageously expensive. He hated it anyway. He hates all restaurants if they're not serving gray meat, potatoes, and peas. "I'm not paying to look at people. I'm paying to eat," he says, staring at the diminutive, artfully arranged plate of mole-braised short ribs with jalapeño gnocchi. I've always thought John should write a review column called "The Trencherman," where a restaurant is judged not by its food quality, presentation, or fabulousness, but by the size of its portions.

Oh well. I'm no better than John is about this birthday stuff. We really need to get a little more proactive about special occasions. Not that I care about birthdays, really.

March 30, 2003

I meet Alex for dinner at Peter Luger's.

The evening was a Greatest Hits of his life: his friends, his great book-loves, his most miraculous rejuvenations, the women he's kissed and occasionally more. Turns out he's a hypochondriac too, but then, what doctor isn't? All a little TMI for a stranger, but all told in the most captivating manner. We discovered we grew up in adjacent towns, both entitled only children. We love the same writers, comedians, music. He told me he peed once next to Springsteen, "but I never looked down." That showed admirable restraint, I thought. As I had guessed when I met him, he worries a great deal about losing his hair, the firmness of his belly. He showed me pictures of himself as a track star in college. He told me he still had great legs.

He laughed at my jokes.

A mutual friend had told me he was more than a little self-absorbed. I'm not quite sure if he remembers my full name or the names of my children; I think he got the name of my dog. But what's there to know about a middle-aged woman who spends her life catering to two babies? He was funny enough to do stand-up, he liked Jewish girls, he adored his father, and he'd been on *The Today Show.* More than once. And when he talked about his daughter, his whole face changed. He became lighter, younger. He wasn't a perfect husband, obviously, but in this way at least he was on the side of the angels.

For my birthday he gave me a mug advertising a surgical compression garment and an awful red canvas tote he picked up at a fund-raiser. It read, "Politics is my bag." One couldn't be seen carrying it anywhere but the Upper West Side. I loved it. "It's all about your pleasure," he said. And it was.

"Can I get a kiss in return?" he asked.

What's one silly kiss? Hey, it's my birthday.

March 31, 2003

Today I get, by messenger, on a slip of paper clipped out of a magazine, a quote by Erica Jong: "Monogamy is impossible among interesting people."

Now that's not playing fair. As if I don't worry enough that I'm an old bore whose husband dislikes her and everything she stands for. Screw this guy and his sixties baby-boomer gestalt. I crumple the paper and throw it away.

April 1, 2003

OK, I've made an appointment for a physical.

No, I haven't! Ahaha! April Fool's!

Shit.

April 7, 2003

Alert the authorities: at eighteen months and two weeks Gus has finally started walking. We're all staring at him like we've never seen a child walk before. And given how skinny he is, and how he totters, he sort of looks more like a meerkat than a human. He'll get halfway down the hall, realize he hasn't fallen, then stop, clap, and shriek *yay* so loudly the neighbors' doors all pop open to see what the hell the commotion is.

He's driving Henry crazy though. You know how you see kids on skateboards grab the back of taxis in NYC traffic to

get a little speed going? That's what Gus does to Henry. He's
not very fast or stable yet, so he'll grab the back of Henry's
shirt as Henry's whizzing by and just sort of use him to pick
up speed. After a few steps Henry ends up with Gus clinging
calmly to his back, as Henry bellows in frustration. For
someone so tiny, Gus is surprisingly hard to shake off.

Henry does have his own form of retaliation though.
Obsessed with combs, he's managed to find and hoard every
comb in the house. When he knows I only want him to carry
one or two (though God knows why; is there going to be a
worldwide shortage of cheap plastic combs?), he hides the
rest down Gus's back. If I leave them alone for a few minutes
and hear a shrill cry, I know I'm coming back to a Gus who
suddenly has perfect military posture, thanks to the sudden
pressure of half a dozen combs pressing against his vertebrae.

April 8, 2003

I don't think anyone really knows who their children are
before they're three. You think you know, but you don't.
Having said that, I will predict that Gus will become
president of his drama club. He gave an Oscar-worthy
performance yesterday. But to understand its import, you
must understand the Key Park.

The Key Park is a children's playground owned by NYU
that is supposed to be for children of NYU faculty and

community residents. It is arguably the nicest, cleanest, least crowded playground in lower Manhattan. It is also, for reasons never fully clear to me, harder to gain admission to than Collegiate. It is controlled by a bureaucrat in one of NYU's real estate management offices who gives out keys by whim, a woman I know nothing about. But as my frustration has grown I have become fond of ascribing to her new identities and new levels of insanity. Most recently I decided she was someone who owns many, many parakeets.

But I digress.

For the last two years I have done everything to get a key to the Key Park. First I put my name on the waiting list months before Henry and Gus were born. I then went into the office every couple of months to ask about where I was on the waiting list. But then I heard that the waiting list was an invention, that people got in according to the Parakeet Lady's whim. So then I walked into the management office and offered to make "a donation" to one of the secretary's favorite charities. (I would have offered the same bribe, only bigger, to the Key Nazi herself, but I could never get in to see her personally.) I tried to get Orma to buy the key from other nannies. At one point I actually called my assemblywoman and protested my right as a community resident to get into the park. The keys, by the way, cannot be copied, and they are guarded like plutonium;

people tend to wear them around their necks. And do not think you can get a kindly person in the park to let you in. People in the park will not let other people in, for fear of losing their Key Park privileges.

So finally, in desperation, I got Irene, Gus's occupational therapist, to write up a letter: "Gus and his brother were born very prematurely, impacting on his typical motor development and hypersensitivity to touch, which also affects his tolerance to crowded places. Play is particularly important to his development, and the Key Park is ideal, as it is generally less crowded and hectic than Washington Square. He tends to shut down and cry when too many children are running around, hindering an opportunity to explore optimally and play with the park equipment..." It went on like this for two pages. It's all true, but that is not the point. The point is that I have become one of the pushy, entitled mothers I have mocked for years.

I took the letter, and I got Gus dressed up in a little snowsuit and hat which are about three sizes too big on him and the wrong color for his olive skin, making him look particularly tiny and wan. (Not that he needs much help.) I did not take Henry—huge, robust, peachy-skinned Henry, who looks like he could single-handedly rearrange the playground equipment. I rolled Gus over to the real estate office, handed over the letter to an assistant, and tremblingly explained our plight. (I really was trembling by this point. I'd worked myself up into quite a state about it.) The Key Woman's assistant curled her lip when she saw me. She began to recite her speech about the waiting list, how despite the fact that I'd been waiting two years, there were still twenty-nine people ahead of me. And they only gave out a few keys a year...

But then the assistant took a hard look at Gus. He was sitting there solemnly, not saying a word, brows knit in his habitual expression of worry. Her lips pursed, and she disappeared.

Twenty minutes' worth of discussion with the unseen Key Nazi later, the secretary returned. She announced with great ceremony that my request for a key had been "granted."

I turned to Gus and said, "Honey, guess what? You're getting a key to the Key Park!" On cue, my heretofore silent child screamed, "*Yaaaaayyyyy!!*"

Now, if I use a certain tone of voice with Gus and say, "Honey, guess what? I am going to feed you to a school of piranha!" he will also shriek, "Yay." But the secretary did not know this. Suddenly she became a human and went on about how nice it will be for Gus and his brother, and they'll meet new little friends *whose parents are professors* (this point emphasized), and so on. Gus burbled away happily for a few moments, and then we got ready to leave. At that point she reached out to shake his hand. Gus pulled away, screaming, like she'd just stabbed him with an ice pick.

"The therapists are working on that," I whispered. "You know—his hypersensitivity to touch."

"Ohhh, that's right, I'm so sorry, I forgot," she whispered.

Never before or since has Gus pulled away from anyone's hand like that. I am so proud.

April 11, 2003

Am I too touchy? Am I? Huh? Orma has something to say about everything I do: what I feed the children, what toys I buy them, what they should wear. Last week my sin was lemonade. "I never see other mothers give their child that," she sniffs.

"Well, you don't see other mothers giving their kids cigarettes either," I say, opening a fresh pack for Henry.

(OK, maybe I'm just working my way up to saying that. But isn't it enough that I thought it?)

Today I was running around, trying to get myself together to visit a friend who just had twin girls. I'm bringing boxes of Chinese food, because she has a hankering and she's so sleep-deprived, ordering take-out seems like one task too many. And then I'm rummaging through all my baby stuff, trying to get some of the girlier items to give her. Orma sees me doing this and says, "When you visit someone who just had babies, you can't bring used clothes! You have to give them new things."

Now, as it happens, the night before I'd found Stephanie's baby registry and sent her cute new outfits. But I loved getting used clothes, Stephanie had *asked* for them, and anyway, what the hell? I wasn't aware I'd hired Emily Post to care for my children.

I just lost it. I was close to tears. I spent that night playing out scenarios in my favorite sci-fi fantasy, whereby Orma's body shows up to work with me, and Henry and Gus, who love her, never notice that I have managed to replace her brain.

When I calmed down I realized that Orma's criticism wasn't really about me. It was about the other nannies. These are the people she answers to, and if it got back to anyone that her employer gave used clothing as a present . . . well! Her stock would go down.

New York nannies, I've discovered, are as competitive in their own way as momzillas. A good employer spends money lavishly not just on the nanny herself but on her children. I would think that nannies, many of whom grew up with very little themselves, might be disgusted by the materialistic, overindulged New York child. *Au contraire.* To the nannies of Manhattan, their child cannot have too much; it's the *other* children who are spoiled.

And woe to the nanny whose charge is not spotless and in blooming health. There is talk. Last week, on my watch, Henry took a header into the ground, cutting up his face and nose. "Make sure that doesn't happen again," Orma says. "I don't want to have to answer anyone's questions."

It's bad enough I feel compelled to keep up with the other mothers. Now I realize I have to help Orma keep up with the other nannies.

I sent Stephanie another present. Just to be on the safe side.

April 12, 2003

"Quick, hit the fast-forward," I scream at John. But it's too late. The enemy has been spotted, the damage done. I had forgotten to warn my husband about Gus's latest fear, a terror so all-consuming that only a ten-ounce bottle and raft of cheddar Goldfish can calm him down. Gus lives in mortal dread of Lena Horne. Now, in the normal course of a man's day, Lena Horne does not figure prominently. But if you are a nineteen-month-old man deeply committed to a *Sesame Street* video called *Learning about Letters,* and a certain septuagenarian songstress is belting out the ABC song with a dozen felt puppets, you must confront this fact of life: Lena happens.

"Why didn't you tell me?" John hisses, as he cradles his

sobbing son in his arms. To Gus John croons softly, "Yes, sweetheart, of course she's frightening. She looks like she eats people."

For reasons best known to himself, John is considerably less sympathetic to Henry's current object of terror, a plush sun with a leering (the less sensitive might say "smiling") face: touch the sun's rays and it plays Mozart. Henry's byword for all things scary is not *avoid*, but *confront and destroy*: like Superman heroically trying to rid the world of kryptonite, Henry, screaming, will grab the sun and try to hurl it out the window. John finds this amusing. I finally had to hide the damn thing, because when Henry was being particularly obnoxious John would dangle it in front of his face and hum the overture from *The Marriage of Figaro*.

What is it with kids and their weird fears? I have one friend who had to abandon an expensive, carefully planned vacation on a dude ranch: her three-year-old, who would pore over pictures of horses, refused to come out of his room when faced with the real thing. Another friend's two-year-old daughter was so scared of the dark she could only sleep with all the lights in her room turned on full blast; I always thought she'd be able to get a tan while she dozed.

Childhood fears, of course, are normal. At various points in their development many if not all kids will be frightened by something: animals, noises, strangers, darkness, as well as certain threats like the possibility of getting lost or the thought of being sucked down the drain in the bathtub.

I just wish Henry and Gus would find a fear and stick with it. The things that set their hearts racing seem to change weekly, and John and I are forever caught off guard when we discover that the pleasant little foray to the Botanical Garden has now become an exercise in damage control, as Henry, normally a plant lover, tries to attack an orchid that apparently *must be stopped before it takes over the Earth*. Or we find we're getting more exercise than we bargained for when Gus refuses to enter an unfamiliar elevator or, as he thinks of it, The Moving Coffin That Whisks You to Oblivion. The next week, unbeknownst to us, Henry and Gus have moved on to dreading something else, while John and I are still having conversations like, "No, we can't take Gus to visit Johanna. Don't you remember? *She lives on the twenty-fifth floor.*"

Watching your children struggle with their fears brings you back, quite forcefully, to your own. Like many children I had a tendency to anthropomorphize everything. I knew, beyond any doubt, that the vacuum cleaner was going to suck me into its gaping maw. If I opened the closet there it would be, blinking and ready to wheel out and overtake me at a moment's notice. But as soon as my mother returned to the room it would scurry back to the closet and pretend to be inanimate. I also knew that the windshield wipers on my parents' car were skinny, beady-eyed ghouls with waving tentacles that were mocking me. The moment I let my guard down, they would reach into the back seat of the car and stab me through the stomach. I still remember carrying on so loudly in a blinding rainstorm that my parents had to drive five miles an hour with the wipers off, my mother's head out the window, shouting reassurances to my father that we were not destined for a head-on collision with a semi.

Of course, there are some fears that reportedly stay with children—and stay with us as adults. I've wondered whether we teach these things to our kids, or whether there is something in the DNA. I do not recall conveying to my baby that it is deeply awful to touch sand, that gooey substances on your hands must immediately be washed off; nor do I remember the conversation where I told him that anything having to do with the circus—clowns, trained bears, people being shot out of cannons, the cotton candy that always finds its sticky way onto your person—is the stuff of nightmares. Yet all the things that give me the shivers have the same effect on Gus.

I feel duty bound to rid Gus of my own little terrors and aversions. So if you see an aged mother and small, skinny boy crouching on the edge of a sandbox, trying to have a good time but in fact cowering while wearing shoes and socks and gloves, please say hello to us! We'll be glad to meet you!

April 13, 2003
So I walk in the door at 5:30 today, feeling almost human. After barely leaving my house for two weeks—work, babies, Orma squabbles, guilt for nagging extramarital thoughts— I finished one troubled, perhaps doomed, article and decided to treat myself well: hair coloring, pedicure, waxing. As I open the door, Henry is on the couch flailing rhythmically, his eyes rolled back into his head. Orma is on the phone with the 911 operator. *"I prayed you'd come and you're here,"* she said, as she threw the phone at me and grabbed Henry, who luckily had not fallen off the couch. Lucky, too, that I came back at that moment, because poor Orma was so upset she couldn't remember my address to tell the EMS workers.

As I talk to EMS I feel his forehead, and he's on fire—which is not so bad. Chances are it's a febrile convulsion and not, say, an epileptic seizure. By now Orma is running back and forth in the hall wailing *"Don't die, my love, don't die!"* *"Don't die"*: not so helpful, and bound to get the attention of the neighbors. Then, when all the neighbors have been sufficiently alerted, she comes back in and starts dousing him with tepid water— which is exactly what she should be doing, except that she was so overzealous about it I was pretty sure for a moment there that he *was* going to die, not from convulsions but from drowning. He had long ago stopped convulsing and was limp and whimpering. Also good, as I kept trying to explain. We gave him Motrin. The EMS people came, we got in the ambulance and went to the hospital; one of the EMS women, so sweet, was telling me about her IVF misadventures and how now she was trying to adopt. Henry just lay there and sucked oxygen, a sweet doughy lump of babyflesh in my arms.

At the St. Vincent's pediatric emergency room, it seems it was a night for running into coffee tables. No fewer than three toddlers had huge gashes in their foreheads from doing exactly that.

With Henry they did all the usual tests and he was so zonked he didn't protest. His fever was 105, even after the Motrin. I knew he'd be fine when, after they finally got the fever down, he methodically shredded an entire box of Kleenex (murmuring, under his breath, "A-choo. Aaaaa-choo"), then began pointing at the heart monitor and going, "On? Elmo? El-*mo?*" apparently in the hopes that the annoying beeping machine would reveal itself to be a television and produce his best friend.

Orma, who stayed home with Gus until we located John, was still babbling by the time she left here. She is wonderful; she cares so much, but it is not good that between the two of us *I'm* the voice of reason when my kid is having to be rushed to the hospital.

The moral of the story? Never go out and have a pleasant day *or your child will have a seizure.*

Of course the moment Orma walked in this morning she said, "Do you think Henry's been brain-damaged?" Gee, thank you, that thought never occurred to me, and at 8 A.M. Monday morning I know it'll cheer me for the rest of my work week!

April 15, 2003
This afternoon I'm taking Gus and Henry for their eighteen-month checkup. For Henry it's a routine exam. For Gus it's like the SATs: it's a day that could determine his future. If he has fallen further off the growth chart, we are going to have to Do Something. I hate having to Do Something, particularly if it involves doctors and needles and pain for my little boy.

Every time I thought about these tests, I would panic at the myriad possibilities. What if Gus needed to be on a special diet for the rest of his life? What if he needed to be prescribed growth hormones—thousands and thousands of dollars and injections every day, for years? I tossed and turned all last night, mulling over the possibilities.

FIRST, THE GOOD NEWS: at almost nineteen months Gus is on the short side but tall enough: at least he won't be starring on a remake of *Fantasy Island*. But he weighs only eighteen pounds. The blood tests have long scary names— alpha-1 antitrypsin, celiac gliadin—and our pediatrician says my featherweight child will have to take them.

April 19, 2003

After extensive tests to determine what's wrong with Gus, the results are finally in. Diagnosis: scrawny. They can't find anything wrong with him. I was telling this to the pediatric ophthalmologist I was visiting today, who was examining Gus to see if he had a lazy eye. He asked if there was any reason for his small size. "The blood tests say he's a shrimp!" I say merrily—and then notice I'm staring down at a man who if he's lucky is five three and a hundred pounds. Seeing the mortification on my face, he quickly replied, "Well, Gus is going to have to marry an Amazon like I did, to counterbalance things genetically." I love this doctor.

And as it turns out, Gus doesn't have a lazy eye, but he's already nearsighted. That intense, slightly cross-eyed gaze I love so much? Not so much a passionate soul trying to make himself known as a guy who's trying to see farther than five inches from his nose. In a couple of years he'll need glasses. Between the tininess, the glasses, the orthotics he wears to correct duck toes and, undoubtedly, the braces, I better start looking into karate classes for three-year-olds.

Anyway, it's too early to tell what his height will be, but now there's talk of giving kids human growth hormone if they don't have a deficiency but are simply short. John—who claims to have once scaled the heights of five nine, but is now lucky to make five seven—is all for it. He feels he suffered as a shortish man, both professionally (a bass in opera is usually a priest, a king, or the devil, and you can't be an imp if you're supposed to be the Prince of Darkness) and personally.

Me, I'm not so sure. Nature has become far too malleable, the handmaiden to nurture. This makes for more dilemmas than I personally bargained for. How much is medical meddling for my boy's health and how much about our collective social vanity?

The hell with it. I'm keeping my list of fabulously sexy, scrawny/short guys, and I'm giving it to Gus on his eighteenth birthday. Mick Jagger, Al Pacino, Ewan McGregor, Robin Williams.

Humphrey Bogart. Need I say more?

April 20, 2003

Beep. Hi, Judith and John, Ultimo Construction here. Salvatore wanted me to tell you he does *understand that the space you're living in with two small children isn't . . . healthy, and he's so sorry Henry climbed out of his crib and turned on the television and was watching infomercials in the middle of the night. Lucky he didn't have your credit card, haha! And in answer to your question, no, usually a job like this doesn't take ten months. This has been a doozie! But Salvatore gives you his word you'll be able to move into your new space soon. Pretty soon. And as soon as we get your next check, that will speed everything up. And we're sorry there was a little problem with the tiles, but it happens all the time. You think you have more than enough, and then . . . anyway, let me check the notes here, the wait for the new tiles is only . . . oh. OK then! Looking forward to getting the check!*

April 21, 2003

Finally got to the doctor's, for a mammogram, anyway. It's taken me years to work up the courage to come here. And I had to hear this.

"I don't love what I see," says the doctor, staring at a sprinkling of white flecks on the shadowy picture of my breast. "It might be nothing," she adds hastily, when she notices the blood drain from my face. "Maybe some calcifications. But I'd like to do a biopsy to make sure."

When does she want to be sure? Tomorrow? Right now? Outwardly I'm calm and nodding, but inwardly I'm thinking *lop them off right now.*

This isn't supposed to happen. One of the good things about marrying John was that there would be one scenario I could cross off my vast list of hypothetical demises. After all, I reasoned, what are the odds he'd have *two* wives with breast cancer? It's like the old joke about the guy who carries a toy bomb on a plane, because the chances of someone else having a bomb are pretty small.

John's leaving for England in a few days. If I tell him I'm having a biopsy, he stays home. Do I want him to stay home? Not like this.

For once in my life I keep my mouth shut.

April 22, 2003

Alex emails, feeling terribly guilty for not having been in touch. Funny; here I was, under the impression that I'd shown remarkable forbearance in not writing or calling, and all the while he's assumed he's been ignoring *me*. Why is that so annoying? Never mind. I'm writing a piece on transsexuals and I need to clarify a few questions about their reconstructive surgery. Yes. Alex can tell me! And I can expense the magazine. So in fact I *need* to see him.

OK, no, I don't.

John will be in England again for Mother's Day. I felt too stupid telling him I wanted him here; after all, is this sentimental slob the person he married? We had a lovely night together. "Will you miss me?" I ask, pathetically. "How can you ask that?" he says, stroking my hair. How can I not?

This time I don't ask if he'll miss Henry and Gus.

April 25, 2003

Before he goes John leaves me with three Mother's Day cards—one from Henry, one from Gus, and one from the dog.

Alex calls. Do not go out with him.

April 26, 2003

Do not go out with him.

April 27, 2003

Do not go out with him.

April 28, 2003

I decide to open John's Mother's Day cards a little early. The one from Henry begins, "Congratulations—You're now a servant."

The one from Gus starts off, "You've managed to survive till another Mother's Day, and that's pretty good going for an old lady. It's sad to have to watch you flounder around in a ham-fisted way, but I'm sure you'll catch on eventually."

I know John thinks he's being funny.

I didn't open the card from the dog.

I go to my email. Alex has written. A few days ago I'd written him a note that began, "I think every inch of you is lovely, but . . . I just can't." Today he's written back, "Yeah, but you haven't seen my best eight inches."

OK, go out with him, but only somewhere where everyone knows the two of you.

April 29, 2003

That was fantastic. Do not go out with him again.

Or if you do, go someplace dark.

April 30, 2003

Biopsy. Not nearly as painful as I thought. And I won't be experiencing any pain in the near future, as I plan to spend the next few days while I wait for the results drunk.

But not with *him*.

SCREW IT, you might be dead next year.

Just one more evening, in the dark place. With good drinks.

May 1, 2003

Henry and Gus are very young. If I switched husbands now, would they even know the difference? Maybe I'd just never mention it! Why do they have to know every little thing I do with my life? I'm their parent; they're not mine!

And it was just a kiss. A few kisses. That's not so bad. People who have been married a long time should be able to kiss other people. Perhaps a certain number of make-out sessions with others should be allotted per year. Like, I don't know, four. Quarterly.

What's bad is not so much the kiss, but what I want to do. What if we redefine it? It wouldn't be sex. It would be more like... New and Improved Second Base!

May 2, 2003

Here's the thing about having an affair. Calling it a low-down dirty betrayal of the person you love is missing the point. No, adultery is a personal insurrection against the oppressiveness of the state. Yes. It's like that culture critic Laura Kipnis says in a book she wrote, *Against Love*: "Adultery is the sit-down strike of the love-takes-work ethic." To have an affair is to protest all that is repressive and stultifying about our society. I wouldn't just be having sex with someone new; I would be striking a blow against the Bush-Rumsfeld-Ashcroft Axis of Evil—against homeland security itself! And I wouldn't just be doing it for myself. I would be doing it for all women who were taken for granted, unappreciated, unloved.

Maybe "unloved" is a little strong. But. Unappreciated, certainly.

May 3, 2003

Woke up this morning covered in hives. Never mind the whole marriage problem; how could anyone ever get naked with a plastic surgeon? Imagine what they're really thinking while they have sex. In their heads they're drawing Magic Marker lines on your thighs.

Besides, this can't be good karma. I don't want to have to *need* a plastic surgeon for anything more serious than a face-lift.

OK, you are never going to have dinner or breakfast or even a Lunchable with that man ever, ever again.

TONIGHT I CALLED JOHN, who's staying with his nephew in Lancashire, and asked him if he had a will. He didn't. "I want you to get one," I said.

"Why, are you in a rush to get rid of me?" he replied.

I ignored this. "Well, *I'm* getting one. We should do this together. At least it's *something* we can do together."

"Why do you want a—" There was a long hissing sound on the phone, then a series of clicks, then a very British recorded voice saying, "Please stay on the line." I realized it was two in the morning in England. Perhaps this could wait until tomorrow.

May 4, 2003

I am going to be alive for the foreseeable future. Must go
back in six months, but the biopsy came back negative.
Henry and Gus will not be out on the street shaking a
Styrofoam cup.

First I said my thanks to God, or maybe the Gods—
whoever happened to be taking my call. Then I kissed
Henry and Gus's sticky little hands. Then I called everyone I
loved just to say hello, but everyone I loved wasn't home so I
left testy messages on their answering machines. Finally,
exasperated, I went on eBay and bid on a really expensive
pair of shoes.

I'll tell John about all this soon. But first I'm going to
live a little. A woman who's been snatched from the jaws of
death has a right, don't you think?

Well, don't you?

May 8, 2003

Last night at the last minute I got a baby-sitter. Alex and I
are to meet for a late dinner. When I am out with Alex I am
not old. I am not anyone's servant. Bonus: my parents would
be pleased I was out with a doctor.

Nine -fifteen, he's late. Nine-thirty, he hasn't shown. I
have a lovely conversation with the chef, who's taking a
break. Ten o'clock, no one's there. Ten-thirty, I go home.

At midnight, I get the call. Alex is not an inconsiderate man; I knew I hadn't simply been stood up. And indeed I'm second in line for calls, after his lawyer and before his wife. There had been an Incident. It had been a tough day at work, a lipo with excessive bleeding, and he needed to wind down a little before he saw me. He spoke quickly, because he was about to be arraigned. I had just one question: how arrogant and self-absorbed do you have to be to light up a joint in front of a couple of cops?

"This is just between us girls," he says grimly, after he's sprung the next morning. "I really can't let this get out."

"So I guess that call to Page Six wasn't such a good idea," I say. Silence. OK, I admit, sometimes my timing is off.

I had another question, but I guess I'll never get an answer. Here I was, new and shiny, a woman to gaze adoringly and hang on every sentence. I'm good at that, better than most. Pamela Harriman and I could have had a gaze-off, and I'd have won. So why was it necessary to light up a doobie before seeing me? A quick drink, maybe; a drink relieves anxiety. Dope alters reality. I thought I wasn't such a bad reality to begin with.

In a few days it'll be Mother's Day. I'll be very happy to see my own mother.

May 10, 2003

John calls tonight to announce he's found a scuffed-up first edition of *Swiss Family Robinson* in an old bookstore in Durham. "Do you think the boys will like it?" he asks eagerly. In about seven years, I say. He presses on: "What have they been doing today?" I tell him. "Bloody pests," he says, with infinite tenderness.

There is a crackle on the phone line, and I imagine a great white shark bumping up against the transatlantic cable. Are there actual cables underwater? Are there great white sharks in the Atlantic? I haven't gotten much sleep lately.

"You still haven't told me why you want a will," John says, a moment later.

"Forget it," I say, knowing I won't. "But we've got to figure something out... If anything ever happens to me, what happens to Henry and Gus?"

"What do you mean?"

"I have no siblings. My parents are too old to take them. My cousins, they've got their own problems. So I've got to pick the right friend. How do you ask someone who's not a blood relative, '*Hey! Want my kids?*'"

"You seem to be forgetting someone."

"No, *you* seem to be forgetting how you've acted most of the time since they were born. I know how you feel about the situation. So help me decide on a friend who—"

"How blind can you be?" John says, his voice rising. "I'm going to be dead when they're still boys. Is this what you want: do you *want* them to become attached to me? Do you *want* them to miss me when I'm gone?"

There are moments when you know what you know. And you know what you know has been wrong.

"Yes, that's what I want," I say quietly.

"If something happens to you," he says, pretending to ignore me, "they will come and live with their father in England. And they will have their auntie Jean and their cousin Gareth. And we will all be fine."

The great white shark is bumping the phone cable again. But then the line clears. "OK," I say. "Fine."

"Fine."

"But just keep thinking about Strom Thurmond."

"He's dead now."

"Pavarotti, then. He's your age exactly."

"Oh, bloody wonderful."

"Larry King..."

"Get a good night's sleep, kiddo."

"Dennis Hopper..."

May 11, 2003

Upstairs, the whining begins around 6:30. Henry lobbying to get up and out, as usual, and saying something about his new favorite object, the spoon. Though he pronounces it "poon." At least, I think that's what he's saying. Isn't it? "Poon." I wonder if I can take one last snooze. The complaining goes on for a minute, only louder.

Then, an ominous silence.

I run upstairs. There is Henry, standing up in his crib, smeared with shit and naked from the waist down. His diaper, as full as a diaper can be, is on the landing of the staircase below.

"Poo," he explains.

But here's the thing. Despite having fallen from a distance of many feet, the diaper has not exploded. It is an intact poo bomb: malevolent, glowering, yet harmless. It is a miracle.

Now, as miracles go, a nonexploding diaper may not rank up there with a vision of the Virgin Mary. But it is Mother's Day, and I'll take my miracles where I can get them. I thought, as I have thought a thousand times since having children, "This could have been so much worse."

I stared at the diaper for a minute. I could have a different life, but I don't. I could love someone else, but I don't. The diaper did not explode. The center held.

In three days my husband, the father of my children, will be home. What can I say?

Reader, I married him.

ON JULY 15, 2003, two weeks before I was to hand in this book to the publisher, I felt queasy. By July 17, I was throwing up. What is the one thing most unlikely to happen to a forty-two-year-old woman who'd spent seven years and $70,000 trying to get pregnant?

Accidents happen.

In fact, I was told by the obstetrician, accidents happen a lot. Older women who've had my kind of history are blithely sure they're impossible, until their bodies tell them otherwise.

I lay in bed, blinded by nausea and indecision for three more weeks. I would take to the streets to protest a woman's right to abortion, and I have, but at this point in my life I couldn't have one myself. In my head the baby—for indeed it was a baby—already had a sex and a name (Elinor) and was looking fabulous in the black and orange of Princeton. I couldn't afford to live in New York with another child, couldn't afford the eight months of nausea ahead of me. And John. How could I afford *that?*

"Admit it, your main goal in life is to kill me off," he said when he heard the news. Then, a little while later, "Just promise me it won't be another boy."

Nature's cruelty can be kind. Old mothers get pregnant, but they have many miscarriages too. I did, and I'm about ninety-five percent glad. I may not be religious, but even in me there is a tiny sliver of belief: that perhaps there are a finite number of souls in the universe, and that if Elinor didn't go the distance in my body, she found another that was more accommodating. And there she grows, perhaps right now.

I have my family. It is complete, and it is mine, and every day I'm grateful.

Not that I don't think about how great it would be if they all moved out of the house for a while.

And speaking of the house, today as I turn in this manuscript I am celebrating the one-year anniversary of the start of my renovation. There have been sightings of Salvatore, somewhat as of a yeti. But so far I am $70,000 poorer and still living in 750 square feet of space with two two-year-olds, a golden retriever, and Orma. And, when he can stand us all, John.